Gallery Management

"Morning Sun," by Rebecca Zelermyer, mixed media, 1974, artist's personal collection.

Gallery Management

REBECCA ZELERMYER

SYRACUSE UNIVERSITY PRESS   1976

Library of Congress Cataloging in Publication Data

Zelermyer, Rebecca, 1919-
   Gallery management.

     1. Art—Galleries and museums—Management.   I. Ti-
tle.
N470.Z44   658'.91'708   76-24790
ISBN 0-8156-0127-1

102271

To

My Darling Husband

William

Whose Patience and Devotion

Enabled Me to Complete this Book

Rebecca Zelermyer has directed her own art gallery for many years and is currently a gallery consultant. She holds a B.F.A. degree from Syracuse University. Mrs. Zelermyer has traveled extensively in Europe and Israel and has presented art shows in New York State, Pennsylvania, New Jersey, and Florida. An accomplished painter herself, she loves every medium and form of art.

CONTENTS

PREFACE

THE PURPOSE of this book is to provide guidelines for
opening and managing an art gallery and to provide instructors with a text that has practical and convenient material
around which a course can be built. The chapters that follow
are intended to give insight into the many ingredients that
add up to a well-planned, smoothly running operation, con-
structed upon a firm foundation.

The experimentally minded instructors teaching
"Gallery Management" in many of the art schools and
universities can easily adapt the lessons of this book to
practical demonstrations in a gallery management course.
For example, if an instructor can find suitable space for an
art gallery—even one room can serve the purpose—and involve students in developing the gallery by actually decorating and furnishing it, selecting the works to be exhibited,
arranging the publicity, setting up the shows, selling the
works of art, and keeping the records, the student will have
had an additional experience that cannot be achieved by
just reading the book. When businessmen say about their
businesses: "You cannot tell much from the outside; you

must come in and look around," it is very true. In setting up a gallery and operating it for a semester or term, the student has more than just the opportunity to "come in and look around"; the student has the opportunity to taste the flavor, feel the substance, and learn to appreciate the nature of the enterprise.

I wish to express my thanks to the following people who have made valuable suggestions which have been extremely helpful toward the completion of this manuscript: Bob Muggleton, The Muggleton Gallery, Auburn, New York; Don Carr, Erie House of Frames, Syracuse, New York; Nan and Howard Miller, The Painters Mill, Rochester, New York; and Jean Richards, The J. Richards Gallery, Inc., Englewood, New Jersey.

Special thanks go to Dr. Alfred Collette, Director, Syracuse University Art Collection, and Mary Ann Calo, Registrar, Syracuse University Art Collection for the opportunity they gave me to work with them and to glean invaluable information concerning many facets of the art field.

I extend my gratitude for his assistance to Charles R. Dibble, Ph.D., Professor of Art and Assistant Dean of the College of Visual and Performing Arts at Syracuse University.

Syracuse, New York   Rebecca Zelermyer
Spring 1976

INTRODUCTION

THERE can be no question in anyone's mind that art in America is now "Big Business." Never before has there been such interest, enthusiasm, and demand for art as in the past two decades. In the early 1960s there were almost five hundred galleries in New York City and by 1970 the count rose to nearly one thousand. You will now find art galleries anywhere you go in this country, from the largest city to the smallest village.

There are so many places selling art today that people who never had any interest whatsoever cannot help but become attracted. Department stores have entered the art business in order to take advantage of what promises to be a profitable field. Sears Roebuck and Company's Vincent Price program has made art a familiar commodity to many people who might never have been exposed to any form of the arts, and Sears is not the only company. There are many others, such as Korvettes and Macy's in New York; Sterns in Paramus, New Jersey; Maas Brothers in St. Petersburg, Florida; Gimbels in both Philadelphia and New York City; Rich's in Atlanta; and Sibley's in Rochester, New York. Restaurants, theatres, banks, and libraries are putting up art displays; even churches, community centers, and synagogues are promoting art exhibitions. Certainly with so much evidence there can be no question that the awareness and the interest, as well as the demand for art has grown since the early 1960s.

It would be nearly impossible to find a complete list of galleries in this country for the simple reason that statistics covering galleries in smaller cities and rural communities do not exist. It is therefore extremely difficult to find out how many there are, how many are successful, and how many are failures. But one thing is certain: the sale of art has developed into a big industry. With this tremendous interest in art many of us who have an art background have considered, at one time or another, opening an art gallery. An honest, sincere gallery director is, in fact, a distinct contribution to the cultural life in a community.

At this point, let me make clear the type of gallery situation at which this book is aimed. I address myself especially to the potential director who plans to open a gallery in a medium- to small-size city or town. And as a corollary to this condition, I also have in mind a gallery that deals in art within a price range not exceeding $1,500.

This type of gallery can perform a fine service by bringing art to the average person in the community who might otherwise never have had an opportunity for exposure to the delights and pleasures of owning fine art. Such galleries actually serve as educational tools in their communities; as a result, both the gallery and the client benefit (incidentally, many art galleries have been known to move beyond the $1,500 price range once they have gained the confidence of their clients). In the process, many clients come to realize that an honest, reliable art dealer can be a most important vehicle for assisting them in building a fine art collection.

As a gallery owner, it is very important to realize from the beginning that one will inevitably be faced with a lot of hard work. There will be times when the work hours will seem excessively and pointlessly long. There will be shows to set up; shows to take down; artists to see and their slides to review; invitations to compose and newspaper articles to write; bookkeeping to do and so on, *ad infinitum* (many of these tasks will be discussed in later chapters). Therefore, it is essential that you have, besides your knowledge of art and your art background, managerial ability. You must treat your gallery as a business enterprise regardless of whether it is to be operated on a full-time or part-time basis.

But most of all, you must love art and you must be willing to share that love with the people who enter your establishment. For this reason, it is tremendously important that you make people feel your gallery is a place where they are free to browse even if they do not make a purchase. You must consider your art gallery as being similar to a retail store. The gallery has a product to sell, and the owner hopes it will attract an individual who is willing to purchase the product. Thus the gallery acts like a retail store as an intermediary between the producer and the buyer. It is in everyone's best interests that the gallery owner be cordial and helpful just as the proprietor of any other establishment that is open to serve the public. Some gallery directors will take exception to this attitude because it is not in keeping with their view of galleries as establishments aimed at attracting the elite, but I would like very much to destroy the concept of art as the exclusive province of the affluent and to dispel the notion that gallery directors are an aloof breed.

When the ordinary person on the street passes an art gallery, there should be no reason to muse: "I'd like to go in there and look around but I guess it's just for the chosen few. It's not for me." Unfortunately, too often a visit to a gallery is an ordeal for the average citizen. Too often a receptionist, perhaps some novice fresh from college with the ink still wet on her B.F.A., looks the visitor up and down with the expression of, "Oh! Another browser!" The poor visitor becomes so self-conscious that he dares not read the descriptive cards below the works of art for fear of revealing ignorance. Overcome by inhibitions, his first reaction is to find the nearest exit and get back on the street. No gallery director or owner can afford to have this happen. The gallery director should try to establish contact not only with the more wealthy and the art connoisseur but also with the general public. The director should attempt to make the gallery a place where everyone feels at home—a place where a person may find new experiences and pleasures.

Gallery owners must, therefore, dispense with the notion that everyone else is interested in the same things they are and should not be oblivious to those who have never been exposed to such cultural experiences. These people can be—and very often are—potential buyers but, because of their reluctance to enter the door of that *sanctum sanctorum,* end up in some other store or decorating shop where they will spend the same amount of money on some expensively framed reproduction or wall fixture.

Gallery directors usually have a point of view (your

gallery should certainly reflect your point of view) but you must, at least at the beginning, keep your ideas flexible. Well-established galleries in New York and in other large cities can afford to be very independent, varying from their point of view not one iota, but the type of gallery being described here cannot afford to be quite so independent. Once you have become well established, you may be able to project your point of view more strongly; you will have achieved a better position to educate your clients, once they have come to rely on your judgment.

Taking this need for flexibility into consideration, it follows, then, that you will have to give a lot of thought to the kind of gallery you want to operate. Some galleries specialize only in one medium of art, such as graphics, oils, watercolors, or sculpture; others offer such forms of art as hand-made jewelry, ceramics, and other handicrafts. You will do well to offer a variety of art forms, especially during the first year of your business, for it will take at least that length of time to learn the types of people your gallery will attract and what types of art are most salable in your area. After a reasonable length of time you will be in a position to make a decision as to which way your gallery will go— what is best suited to you and your clients.

Of course, there is the prospective gallery owner who will say, "I cannot operate a gallery and prostitute myself by catering to the desires of clients. I must project my own point of view. Otherwise I cannot be sincere in my approach." This attitude deserves understanding and respect, but while it may be appropriate for the gallery owner in a large metropolitan city who can attract clients whose interests are similar, such inflexibility can be detrimental to the success and survival of a gallery in a smaller community.

In addition to all these things there is, of course, one thing that cannot be overlooked, without which one cannot consider starting even a lemonade stand. Quite simply, it is *money!* You will need it for rent, insurance, utilities, license fees, taxes, employees' wages, advertising, supplies, repairs, upkeep, equipment, furnishings, lighting, and many other incidentals. It is after all such expenditures have been made that we hope for a reasonable financial return to ourselves as a result of our efforts.

If, after much consideration, you have decided to open a gallery, don't rush headlong into the venture. For a start, visit as many galleries and artists' studios as you possibly can, not only in your own city but in other cities as well. When visiting other galleries, it is a good idea to take notes as to the types of art being shown, the wall coverings against which they are displayed, the room arrangements, the lighting, the fixtures, the manner in which the pieces are hung, the price range of the work, and the names of the artists.

One of the best things you could do would be to try to find a position, even part-time, in another gallery. This would give you the opportunity to learn a good deal about the business, its problems, its needs, and its rewards, after which you would be much better able to make final plans. This situation is not always possible, and, therefore, I hope this book will be able to assist you.

Gallery Management

1

LOCATION

Having decided to open an art gallery, the choice of a location is one of your most important decisions. Begin by asking yourself the following questions:

1. What area will be most convenient for me?
2. What type of property is adaptable for use as a gallery?
3. Should I buy or rent? How much can I afford to pay?
4. What kind of wall space and floor area does the location have?
5. Is there ample parking space?
6. Does the city, town, or village's zoning allow this type of establishment?

Let us go over these points individually.

"Noontime," by Rebecca Zelermyer, mixed media, 1974, artist's personal collection.

1. WHAT AREA WILL BE MOST CONVENIENT FOR ME?

It is axiomatic that your gallery be conveniently accessible from your living quarters, for traveling great distances can prove a chore, especially if you are in an area that experiences bad weather during the winter months. Some galleries, such as The Muggleton Gallery in Auburn, New York, and the East-West Shop in Victor, New York, have living quarters on the same premises as the galleries, and this can very often be an advantage.

2. WHAT TYPE OF PROPERTY IS ADAPTABLE FOR USE AS A GALLERY?

It is not necessary that your gallery be located in a modern shopping center, where the rents are usually high. It is not even necessary that your gallery be located in an area where there is a great deal of foot traffic. As a matter of fact, your gallery may acquire added charm in a converted barn or an old house, in either a suburban or urban area. Old one-room schoolhouses or small old churches often make handsome galleries; these, incidentally, are types of structures which provide a leisurely atmosphere for browsing.

A word or two of caution is in order, however. If you look for a barn, a one-room schoolhouse, or a small church, try to find one located on or near a well-travelled road. Also, if your location is the small church or one-room schoolhouse on a country road, you must be prepared to spend

more money on publicity until your operation becomes
known. Happily, sometimes the rent in these places is less
expensive, thereby making it possible to allot more money
to advertising.

On the other hand it can be an asset if you find a suitable location where there are other specialty shops (antique,
curio, special-interest). People, especially families, very
often like to make a day's outing—if there is no gas shortage;
they will not usually hesitate to travel reasonable distances
to take advantage of opportunities to visit several interesting
shops at the same time.

There are galleries that occupy space in office buildings,
and there are galleries that share a large area with other
shops where, for example, each shop has its own space within the over-all area, and there is no conflict of interests.
Each shop enhances the others.

If you are fortunate enough to find your location in an
affluent to middle-income area that has homeowners, apart-
ment dwellers, and condominiums, you have a ready-made
clientele.

3. SHOULD I BUY OR RENT? HOW MUCH CAN I AFFORD TO PAY?

Regardless of whether you decide to rent or buy, consult a
reputable lawyer before signing any contracts. A good real
estate broker can also be of assistance in helping you with
your location and in helping you make the best arrangements.

It is best, naturally, to invest as little as possible in the beginning, unless money is no object. It usually takes at least a year and sometimes a little longer before you are able to do much more than pay expenses. There are galleries that have been financially successful from the day of their first show, but these are the exceptions. Usually, it is best to rent when you are just beginning, unless, as previously mentioned, money is no object. And, of course, should you happen to select your location in an area where property values are rising, and should you have the money, it could turn out to your advantage to buy rather than rent.

It is extremely difficult to give advice regarding the amount of rent that should be paid, for any assay of such a hypothetical situation will be highly conjectural: if one does so-much and so-much business, naturally, one can afford to pay accordingly. The best advice, taking an overall view, is that you set aside approximately $2,000 for the sole purpose of paying your rent for at least ten months, assuming that you will be paying in the neighborhood of $200 a month. You can normally figure your rent by the standard formula of about 10 percent of your gross business, although if you live at the same place you obviously have a bonus.

There is also the possibility of renting on a percentage basis; in other words you pay the landlord a percentage based on gross sales. With such an arrangement, it is always a good idea to establish a sliding scale—10 percent on the first $15,000 gross sales; 7½ percent on the gross sales of $15-25,000; and 5 percent on gross sales over $25,000. By this formula $40,000 a year in gross sales would dictate a rental of $1,500 plus $750 plus another $750 or a total of $3,000 per year ($250 per month). It goes without saying that the landlord will not be willing to wait for the year to pass before receiving his rent, so the two of you must agree on a certain amount to be paid monthly; at the end of the year either you owe him or he owes you. Of course, in an arrangement of this kind, your sales book and figures must be available to the landlord should he care to check your records.

Make certain that you have complete understanding on what is included in your rental. Heat? Hot water? Electricity? Air conditioning? Snow removal? There are times when these items are included and times when they are not. Do not hesitate to question every possibility.

The ideal situation is one in which the landlord makes all necessary major renovations, but this is seldom the case. You should make every effort to have the landlord paint the exterior of the property, especially for the first time, and insist that the landlord make all the necessary repairs in the parking area and on the pavement in front of the building. If these are in poor condition, you certainly do not want to be subjected to the expense of concrete or blacktop work.

If you have settled on an old barn, a one-room schoolhouse, or a small church, your landlord will probably not be willing to do much. But, as mentioned earlier, the rent in these places is usually less than in other places, so it can be an advantage to make your own investment in repairs. You should get at least three estimates on any major repairs before you commit yourself to any lease.

In any case, you should be reluctant to enter into any agreement in which the landlord does not assume total responsibility for the proper operation of the heating system and the air-conditioning system (if the latter exists). The plumbing and roof should also be his responsibility. In the event that you install the air-conditioning as part of your renovation plan, the air-conditioning unit or units are your responsibility; if new, they will be under a warranty which will relieve you from expense for a reasonable length of time.

4. WHAT KIND OF WALL SPACE AND FLOOR AREA DOES THE LOCATION HAVE?

You must give both wall space and floor space careful consideration because they influence directly very important aspects of your enterprise.

Wall space will govern the size and number of paintings that can be hung at any one time. It is very convenient not to have to clear the walls and move all the paintings to the storage area in order to present a show. Thus it is advantageous, although not absolutely mandatory, that there be enough wall area to be categorized as "Prime Space," with additional space to be considered "Secondary." Prime Space can be devoted to your one-man, one-woman, or group shows; your Secondary Space (if you have more than enough Prime Space) can be used for the other artists who are part of your stable.

Floor area can govern the number and placement of display racks and also determine whether sculpture and ceramic shows will necessarily be confined to small pieces. Floor area is also important if you are planning on selling pottery, jewelry, and general handicrafts. Is there room for shelving for your pottery, either against the walls or free standing? Is there room for a display case? Is there an area that can be used for a reception during an opening? Such an area does not have to be free at all times, but it is nice to be able to move things around so that such an area can become available.

There are still other kinds of space—storage and office —that must be considered. A kitchenette area with stove and refrigerating facilities can be a great convenience. It is vitally important that you have enough behind-the-scenes space, for there will be numerous things that will require storage and even more to be packed and unpacked. It is always possible to keep your desk and file cabinet in a remote corner of your gallery, but it is preferable to have a separate room—no matter how small—for your office. It will give you privacy when working on your records and, even more important, give your clients privacy when they are making arrangements for a purchase.

And remember, of course, that a washroom is not only an essential; in most locations it is a legal requirement.

5. IS THERE AMPLE PARKING SPACE?

Parking space is almost always a problem, especially so where an older residential area has been rezoned commercial. The space for cars at your gallery during a normal business day need not be very big, since you will probably have only three or four customers at a time. However, during openings it would be ideal to have more space available, which can be arranged by scheduling openings at a time when neighboring shops are closed—evenings or Sundays, for example.

6. DOES THE ZONING ALLOW THIS TYPE OF ESTABLISH- MENT?

Make certain of one thing—that your prospective gallery is permitted under the local zoning ordinances in effect for the location you have chosen. There is the classic story, complete with the traditional unhappy ending, of the lady who had a great opportunity, or so it appeared at the time. Her close friend lived in a very big old home, the lower level of which was an ideal place for an art gallery. There was a separate entrance, right off the street, leading directly into the lower level; the house was only two blocks away from "Gallery Row," several blocks of special-interest shops, sculpture galleries, craft shops, and a very successful gallery showing only abstract paintings. What could be better? An arrangement was made to lease the lower level on a percent- age basis. A great way to rent any space! No business, no rent! The entrepreneur invested about $2,500 in fixtures, lighting, carpeting, and all the other necessities for decorat- ing a handsome gallery. She arranged an elaborate cham- pagne opening. The place was packed with visitors on open- ing night.

Unfortunately, cars parked on nearby streets attracted the attention of the area residents, and complaints came pouring into City Hall. Even though the gallery was only two blocks north, on the same street as "Gallery Row," this block was not commercially zoned. Her appeals fell on deaf ears, and she was given six months to close her doors. It was a most unpleasant experience.

No matter how attractive the location, do not rely on winning the case if a zoning ordinance is in question. It's not worth the risk.

2

DECORATING, FURNISHING, LIGHTING

You are the only judge of just how much you can afford to spend on decorating, but one rule-of-thumb is to spend the minimum to achieve the desired results. A simple, dramatic plan is in better taste than a gaudy one and will invariably provide a better showcase for the contents of the gallery.

First select the color scheme you plan to use in decorating the gallery and then coordinate the colors for the walls, carpeting, and fixtures around this scheme.

WINDOW TREATMENT

Before becoming completely involved in carpentry and painting, it is a good idea to give considerable thought to the window arrangements. If there are too many windows depriving you of wall space, it is a good idea to close up some of them with masonite or wall-board, then cover them in the same manner as you cover the rest of your walls. Natural light, however, can be an advantage, so do not obstruct the light from the windows you decide to retain. These windows can be simply and effectively decorated with shutters which can be kept open during the day and closed during the evening, thus adding to the gallery's security. If shutters prove too costly, a simple drape is appropriate.

WALL COVER

Some walls may be covered with burlap and others with pegboard, for these two backgrounds are attractive and versatile. The following incident, incredible as it may seem, should sound a warning, for these things do happen: A friend, in her eagerness to get her gallery ready for its opening, nailed the pegboards directly to the walls! No back space for pegboard hooks! Her reaction, when she started to hang paintings, was indescribable. Be sure you have one-inch furring strips attached to the walls at eighteen-inch intervals before you put up your pegboards, preferably the kind with one-eighth inch holes, since it is a little less commercial-looking than the sort with quarter-inch holes.

LIGHTING

The lighting is perhaps the most important aspect of your gallery. Proper lighting not only enhances paintings and objects, it also creates dramatic effects. In most instances, track lighting is the simplest method of distributing illumination exactly where it is needed. Its installation is not usually costly, and it can be done without major alterations.

According to Carol L. Crane, in the November 1973 issue of *American Home*, "Track lighting is, in essence, a system whereby an electrified track—actually a long, continuous outlet—is installed on ceiling and/or wall to receive individual swivel lights that can be positioned anywhere along the length of the track." It is relatively simple to change the point of focus and to change the position of the lights on the track. One can light up a large area as well as a focal point. The lamp holders come in sizes that hold bulbs anywhere up to 100-watts, occasionally even larger. There are many styles, shapes, sizes, colors, and designs, so shopping for this item very carefully before making a final selection can be very rewarding. Track lighting is available through most electrical wholesalers and leading manufacturers such as Lightolier, Swivelier, and Thomas Industries; these are only a few of the large manufacturers, and there are also smaller companies that make a very satisfactory product.

FLOOR COVERING

There is really no substitute for carpeting. It is actually cheaper to maintain and it gives the gallery a warmth that cannot be achieved by any other floor covering. The best of all possible choices is indoor-outdoor carpeting, now available in practically every color and pattern that one could possibly want. Furthermore, it is extremely easy to

31

care for; in the event of spills, it can be wiped up as simply as any linoleum floor. Buy a medium quality, buy it from a reliable source, and if at all possible, do have the carpet dealer install it for you.

SHELVING

If you are planning a line of pottery, ceramics, and small sculpture, it is very nearly imperative to have an interesting grouping of shelves. These can be designed in a variety of materials, such as wood, metal, and plastic. Wood and metal shelving have been around for a long time, and there is no doubt that this type of shelving is suitable, but the use of rigid plastics has, in recent years, made esthetically pleasing pieces available at reasonable prices.

The French etagere or whatnot is now available in a very good quality polymer molded to resemble bamboo, wicker, or some other design. This type of material will neither chip nor peel, has excellent durability, and can be purchased in several combinations of sizes. It is so sturdy that it need not be attached to walls and can be used free-standing not only for room dividers but also for uniform or step arrangements. It comes unassembled and can be easily put together.

SHELVING FOR STORAGE AREA

You will need some inexpensive shelving for this area. There are numerous supplies to be stored, such as tissue paper and boxes for packing, office supplies, display supplies, and sundries. Together with this you will need space for your ceramic pieces that are kept on hand as backup inventory. This inexpensive shelving is readily available in almost any discount store. It is metal shelving that you assemble yourself and it is adequate for the purpose.

PEDESTALS

It is a good idea to have several pedestals of different heights for displaying important pieces of sculpture or ceramics. Variously sized sewer pipes make interesting pedestals, and wooden boxes covered with burlap can also be very attractive. But make certain that the taller ones are adequately weighted with bricks or large stones! One should also exercise a certain amount of discretion in their placement about the gallery, for they can be highly vulnerable in traffic lanes.

DISPLAY RACKS

Graphics call for special display racks, of which two types are preferable. One is the rack that stands directly on the floor and holds the graphics rather like a large file folder, one graphic in front of the other. The customer can easily flip through them. For limited floor space there is another type of rack that is bolted to the wall, much like a big book whose pages may be turned by the potential customer.

33

Plastic envelopes for graphics should be used with floor racks for customers will actually be handling the merchandise. These envelopes are available in sizes ranging from 10 x 12 inches to 24 x 36 inches. They are made of clear plastic, some with black binding around the edges. (Usually the art firms that sell graphics also sell the plastic envelopes and graphic racks.)

If you are using the wall rack, it would be advisable to have the graphics matted and covered with cellophane. It will take a little ingenuity to hang the graphics on the rack "pages." One trick is to use a stick-on hanger, placing it on the back of the mat, and then hanging the piece with a ¾-inch brad. For large graphics the floor rack is the better of the two; otherwise the graphic will exceed the dimension of its mount.

It cannot be overemphasized that, regardless of how they are displayed, graphics should not be displayed *unless they are properly protected.* They *must* be either covered with cellophane or put in plastic envelopes, for it is amazing how quickly graphics become shopworn without protection.

MANAGEMENT ESSENTIALS

Outside, there must be a sign to identify your gallery, and inside, stationery, business cards, and receipt books. The design for these four items should be coordinated, especially in regard to type of print, information, and logo. If you find these four items too costly, omit the printed receipt pads and substitute a salesbook in duplicate at a stationery or office supply store. Order a rubber stamp with the gallery name, address, and phone number, and then you can stamp both copies of your receipt forms. At some later date you can have your salesbook imprinted with your personal information.

If you are selling pottery, small sculpture, jewelry, etc., it is important to have several different sizes of paper boxes and tissue paper for packing these objects. At a later date these also can be imprinted especially for your gallery. Cardboard tubes are a necessity for unframed and unmatted graphics, and it is also a very good idea to have a supply of different sized plastic bags. Even a painting should be protected when the customer leaves the gallery with it.

Open a checking account and have your checks imprinted with your gallery name and address.

Arrange for your phone or phones.

Don't forget your guest book! You can buy one or have one made to order for your gallery. Keep your guest book and pen in a prominent place in the gallery. It is very important that visitors sign the guest book. Not only does it provide the basis for developing a mailing list, but the signatures and comments of your guests also constitute a record of gallery activity that can be an invaluable source of information.

If possible, it is a good idea to get a bulk-mailing permit through the post office. Once your mailing list is built up, a bulk-mailing permit can save money.

Buy a good hand viewer for slides. Usually an artist will submit slides or photographs of paintings when calling on you for the first time.

OFFICE AND HOUSEKEEPING SUPPLIES

You will need a desk and chair for your office, and it is a good idea to have a few chairs (try to find interesting ones) placed around the gallery.

You should have a filing cabinet, preferably one with two or three drawers, and several card file boxes and file cards. You will also want a cash box to hold money and sales slips.

You will need all the usual supplies in two categories, labeling and installation. For labeling you will need price tags, scotch tape, masking tape, and marking pencils. For installation you will need picture wire, screw-eyes, a yard-stick, touch-up for frames, scissors, and stapler.

You should have several wastepaper baskets, an electric broom or vacuum cleaner, and a good supply of dust cloths. These items suggest menial activities, indeed, but a sloppy, dusty gallery leaves an immediate bad impression in the visitor's mind.

RECEPTIONS

While it may not be absolutely essential, it is highly advisable that you own the few things needed primarily for the opening days of the one-person or group shows. There will be intermittent need for a fifty-cup coffee maker, a large punch bowl, a folding table (30 x 72 inch is a good size), and a collapsible coat rack. You can also use a few platters for cheese and crackers and a few small dishes for nuts. And always purchase paper coffee cups, plastic punch glasses, napkins, and doilies in quantities of five hundred, for there is a great saving when these paper items are bought in large quantities. Incidentally, do as much buying as possible from wholesale sources when setting up the gallery. As the owner or director of a commercial enterprise, you are entitled to wholesale prices wherever possible.

One final admonition, distasteful as it may be: Keep ashtrays around. Many people still smoke and will think nothing of extinguishing their cigarettes on your carpeting, in your flower pots, and on your table tops.

And now we have nearly everything except ART.

3

ACQUIRING INVENTORY

A list of artists whose work you would like to have in your gallery should be compiled long before renovating and decorating begins. Arrangements for the acquisition of art and the setting up of your gallery should be done simultaneously, for the one will influence the other. The gallery may be completely decorated and furnished, but before the first client walks across the threshold, there must be a collection large enough to convince the client that you are really and sincerely operating an art gallery.

There are many places where you can make contact with artists. You will find outdoor art shows all over the country. These are excellent places to meet many artists and see their work. Boston's annual show is a fine example of this type of "clothesline" exhibit, and New York's Washington Square show, even though not as fine as the Boston exhibition, is another example.

Most museums have regional shows once a year. These are usually juried by knowledgeable judges, and as a result, only the best pieces of those submitted are exhibited. Don't miss these shows when they are in your area. As a matter of fact, it is worth traveling to nearby cities to view these exhibitions. If you find works that interest you in these regionals, the museum will gladly give you the information you need in order to contact the artists personally.

The Whitney Museum of American Art, 945 Madison Avenue at 75th Street, New York City and The Philadelphia Art Alliance, 251 South 18th Street, Philadelphia, Pennsylvania, have annual exhibitions. Even if you are not near these places you can write and request a catalogue, fine productions that are well illustrated and available at a minimal cost. They will also be very happy to provide you with any information regarding the artists.

Art News, 750 Third Avenue, New York City, usually has a listing at the beginning of the year that tells an artist "When and Where to Exhibit." These listings are nation-wide listings and even though this information is meant to aid the artist, there is nothing to prevent a gallery owner from going to these places to find talent. Another magazine, *The Art Gallery,* Hollycroft Press, Inc., Ivoryton, Connecticut, has an up-to-date monthly report on what is going on in the art world. They list exhibitions in New York City and exhibitions in other parts of the country. You will also find *Arts Magazine,* Art Digest Inc., 23 East 26th Street, New York City, and the magazine *Art in America,* 150 East 58th Street, New York City, extremely useful.

Other fine sources of talent are art schools, both the independent ones and those which are part of a university. Faculty members and graduate students may well turn out to be potential contributors to your collection.

The Art Information Center, 189 Lexington Avenue, New York City, can be very helpful in locating fresh new talent. And you can shop for talent rather easily in large metropolitan cities; you will find galleries usually concentrated in one area, thereby giving you the opportunity to scout many places without traveling great distances. But do not be disappointed if some art dealers are not too anxious to share a good artist, for even if your gallery is located in another city, some gallery directors are not very cooperative.

If the dealers are not willing to help you locate particular artists, you will have to resort to other means to locate those whose work you are really interested in. Unfortunately, you cannot always depend on the phone book, if only because many artists have unlisted numbers. If this is the case, don't give up but let the following experiences urge you on. I have located an artist by writing a letter, addressing it to the gallery exhibiting his/her art, and writing "Personal" on the envelope. I have located artists by tracking them down through other artists. I have traced artists through art clubs, and on one occasion, I placed an ad in the personals column of the local newspaper in the town where the artist lived. She then contacted me.

There is one thing you should always keep uppermost in your mind when searching for artists: *do not* put any importance on age, sex, color, or religion. If the work is good, that is all that counts.

There is a possibility that some artists will call on you when they learn you are opening a gallery; it is a certainty that once you are established they will call on you. Artists realize that gallery owners (also referred to as art dealers and art agents) are very important people. Most artists cannot paint and, at the same time, merchandise their own works. They realize that selling art is best left in the hands

41

of a professional art dealer, agent, or gallery director.

The artists (painters, sculptors, ceramists, and all craftspeople) who contact you will, as a rule, bring either slides or photographs. They realize that there is one thing a gallery owner isn't too anxious to see: an artist with a huge portfolio of his work who wants to set it up all over the gallery at an inconvenient time. Artists know that if a gallery director is interested in what has been seen on the slides, the director will make an appointment either to visit the artist's studio or have the artist bring the originals to the gallery at a time convenient for both the artist and the dealer.

There are a few things that are not always obvious from a slide or a photograph: size, technique, and medium. Make sure, if there is any question, that you ask the artist about these things. Furthermore, do not be too quick to dismiss an artist if the slides are not perfect, inasmuch as slides do not always do justice to the originals. If you feel this might be the case, ask the artist to send you a small sample piece, after which you can make a decision as to whether you will want to handle the artist's work.

There may be times when an artist will want to leave a group of unframed oils with you. This is fine in principle, but do not hang a wall of unframed pieces: raw edges are seldom an asset in selling paintings. To the individual who is knowledgeable and understands art, it really makes no difference, but to the person off the street it is usually a deterrent to buying a painting. You will eventually be able to detect the buyer to whom you can present a piece with its edges raw.

Not only can you acquire your art directly from artists

but you can also buy from firms who represent artists. This type of wholesale representative is more common in the graphics field. The following are a few of the types of wholesaler to which I make reference:

Lublin Graphics
33 East Elm Street
Greenwich, Connecticut

Roten Galleries
123 West Mulberry Street
Baltimore, Maryland

Tomlinson Collection
1330 B. Reisterstown Road
Baltimore, Maryland

You will find these and other dealers like them advertising in some of the art magazines. Once you have established your gallery, you won't need to worry about finding them: their representatives who travel in your area will find *you*.

Some of these firms deal, for the most part, in decorative prints that are keyed to big city selling, so be careful and be very selective. They usually have an exchange program, and it is very important that you determine this as soon as you begin to do business with them. Have an understanding which enables you to exchange a piece, and arrange a time limit for making exchanges. Unlike the artist, who should exchange a piece regardless of the length of time you have had it, the wholesale representative does not always do this.

The wholesale graphics representatives rarely send a portfolio on consignment. It is expected that you pay for the work soon after you receive it. Their discount is usually 50 percent off the list price. Again, don't take it for granted. Ask! Even though these firms do not send work on consignment, they have been known to send a portfolio, on approval, for a two- or three-week period. Some of them will send their salesman directly to your gallery with a huge portfolio for a two-day show.

Graphics can be purchased matted or unmatted, the latter—naturally—costing less; you decide which is best for you. If floor racks are used, then buy graphics unmatted and put them in plastic envelopes. But if wall racks are to be installed, then buy graphics matted and cellophaned unless you plan to mat and cover them yourself. In this case make certain to include the price of the mat in the retail selling price.

If you are planning a line of ceramics and pottery, it is a very good idea to join the American Craft Council, whose address is 44 West 53rd Street, New York City. Do this immediately on deciding to carry a line of crafts, for The American Craft Council is one of the best in the country and their yearly dues are only $10. It is a distinct advantage, especially when first starting in business, to acquire even your ceramics on consignment. Most ceramists prefer to sell outright, but there are some who are willing to work on a consignment basis; you will simply have to seek them out. There are area craft shows that offer an easy means of making contact with these artists; one of the best in the northeast is in Rhinebeck, New York. The Council will give you information regarding most shows and will point out the best ones in most parts of the country.

Jewelry is also an attraction and brings many people into the gallery. However, craftsmen of jewelry—especially those specializing in highly original pieces—are not very prolific, so it is not always possible to get much from them on consignment. If you are near a university with an art school, you may be able to find faculty members who specialize in handmade jewelry. You should be selective and have only the finest handcrafted quality pieces. You *must* shop very carefully for your jewelry, and it must be original, since you are, after all, competing with mass-produced items.

If you find a jeweler who is willing, you can make an arrangement with him for made-to-order pieces. You render your clients a special service when you assist them in designing pieces that are one-of-a-kind and made especially for them. Many young people love to design their own wedding bands and such young people can be developed into serious clients and future collectors of art.

Many galleries refer to crafts as their "bread and butter" line, and indeed, profit in this department has been known to pay the rent when other departments are slow. Pottery has become a very popular all-occasion gift. It is especially popular with the young moderns, a group, incidentally, that you should do everything possible to attract into your gallery. These young people constitute an interested and well-informed group that will become, as mentioned earlier, your future customers.

4

CONTRACTUAL ARRANGEMENTS

Let us now consider the different contractual arrangements for acquiring your art.

You can, as suggested previously, have a consignment arrangement with the artist, which means that you do not pay the artist until the work is sold. Most artists are willing to leave at least a few pieces on this type of trial basis, but make certain the artist does not assume you are willing to provide a one-man show merely because you are willing to accept a few pieces in this manner. When you ask an artist for the first time to leave his work on a trial basis, it is imperative to have a mutual understanding as to how long the pieces will be retained. Two or three months, it would seem, is a reasonable length of time to see how your clients react to an artist's work.

When you have had the opportunity to see how the work sells, you can invite the artist to become a member of your stable or, as some directors put it, "join the roster." Once an artist acquires this status, he is usually willing to leave a goodly number of pieces on consignment. At the time you invite an artist to join your roster, you should get an exclusive from him for your area, a one hundred mile radius—more or less—defining that area.

Commission on consignment pieces can vary from 33 1/3 percent to 50 percent. This applies to paintings, graphics, sculpture, ceramics, jewelry. The artist sets the retail selling price, and your commission is derived from a percentage of this price.

Most artists frame oil paintings, the frames are usually included in the retail selling price of the painting, and commission is calculated on the total selling price. Make sure you have a clear understanding of this with your artists. It is a good idea to have them provide lists that show the prices of paintings both with and without frames, since there are times when a client might hesitate to buy a piece if he dislikes the frame. Neither the artist nor the art dealer would want to lose a sale for this reason. You can easily accommodate the client by removing the painting from the frame and deducting the price of the frame from the cost of the painting.

You will also have artists who use extremely simple (slat) framing, and nine times out of ten these pieces carry the same price with or without the frames. Always check this with the artist. Take nothing for granted. Incidentally, "take nothing for granted" in the art business is a splendid motto. Ask! Ask! Ask! It can spare one much grief.

There may be occasions when a client is very much interested in the work of a particular artist, yet there may be nothing of his in the gallery that is exactly what the client wants. You can always send the customer to the artist's studio, but in instances of this kind you should not expect full commission. For example, if your commission is normally 40 or 50 percent, you should expect no more than 30 percent. It is only fair that some concession be made on the artist's behalf when his time and effort exceed his obligation to the gallery.

There are gallery owners who expect full commission in any case—whether the work is sold in the gallery; whether the client is sent to the artist's studio; or even when a client, residing within the gallery's exclusive area, goes to the artist's studio on his own. In situations of this type, the artist should be given the small consideration mentioned above. In the long run it helps create a closer relationship between artist and dealer in which neither party exploits the other.

You can also buy outright from artists themselves. The following points are some of the reasons in favor of this procedure:

1. If an artist is very popular, he may be independent and unwilling to send the work out on consignment.

2. One sometimes receives a larger discount when buying outright than when doing business on consignment.

3. The artist may live in a foreign country and be unwilling to do business except through straight sales.

4. The work is so good, yet so inexpensive, that you feel you cannot afford to pass it up, and there is no other way to acquire it except by buying outright.

Regardless of any of these reasons, you should buy outright from artists only if you have extra money. I do not recommend putting yourself in a financial bind no matter how tempting and attractive the situation may look. And it is imperative that you have the privilege of exchanging unsold pieces no matter how long you have had them.

As you can see, acquiring inventory takes a great deal of time. This is only one persuasive argument for planning all your shows well in advance of their scheduled openings. You must allow time; make no plans that leave you no breathing space. There is always the possibility that an artist will not get his work out on the exact date promised; there is always the possibility that things may be delayed in transit; and there is always the possibility that things may be lost or damaged in transit.

One cannot be too emphatic in insisting that, whether you buy outright from an artist or from a wholesale representative, or whether you acquire your inventory on a consignment basis, you have firm commitments as to delivery dates and means of delivery. And most of all, make certain those dates are well in advance of the actual dates on which you need the pieces. A week to ten days is "well in advance."

5

INSURANCE, TRANSPORTATION, CONTRACTS

INSURANCE

Insurance premiums are the price you pay to be emancipated from the headaches of loss due to situations not only beyond your control but also situations within your control. If you are adequately insured you will have the security of knowing that even if you suffer a loss you will not be a loser.

There are two forms of insurance coverage that are essential to practically all businesses—fire and theft insurance and liability insurance. And there are other forms of insurance that are desirable though not essential—business-interruption insurance, rent insurance, crime insurance. Consult an honest, reliable insurance broker and arrive at a plan to cover your needs. A good broker can assist you in securing the correct coverage at minimum cost.

The method by which you cover the pieces you hold on consignment requires additional consideration. There are galleries that carry no insurance on works of art consigned to them and there are other galleries that insure consigned work anywhere from 33 1/3 to 66 2/3 percent of value.

There are very few galleries that insure consigned pieces for the full 100 percent because most artists have a policy that insures their work not only when it is in their own studio, but also when it is in a gallery, when it is on approval in a client's home, when it is in a vehicle on the way to a gallery, and when it is in a vehicle on the way to a prospective buyer. A gallery, however, should have a sense of responsibility and find a midway point compatible to both the gallery and the artist. If a consigned piece is stolen, for instance, who's losing what! Not only is the artist losing a piece of work but the gallery is losing the possibility of making a sale. Furthermore, if this loss was due to some negligence on the part of the gallery then the artist's insurance company may consider the gallery liable. It is imperative that you know what insurance coverage your artists carry, and it is just as imperative that your artists know what insurance coverage, if any, you plan to carry on their work. Your insurance broker should work very closely with you on establishing the best possible arrangement for coverage on the pieces you hold on consignment.

TRANSPORTATION

It is usually the artist's responsibility to see that his work is delivered. In many instances this is simply a matter of the artist bringing his work to the gallery. There are, of course, other instances. For example, if a gallery in Los Angeles is very eager to show the work of an artist whose studio is in New York City, and the artist is not so anxious, then the

Los Angeles gallery may have to make some allowance for freight or, depending on how independent the artist is, pay all the freight charges.

If you plan to acquire some inventory from abroad, you will find that artists in foreign countries rarely contribute anything toward shipping charges. I have found several instances when it was worthwhile to pay the freight from abroad because the work was not only very good but also very reasonable in price. In such cases, buy several pieces and arrange to have them shipped at the same time. It usually costs the same amount to ship one piece that it does to ship three or four.

Freight charges can be a big item in your operating budget. Don't treat this expenditure lightly; it can eat away your profits.

CONTRACTS BETWEEN THE GALLERY AND THE ARTIST

The American Collegiate Dictionary defines a contract as: "An agreement between two or more parties for the doing or not doing of some definite thing." According to this definition, a contract could be written or verbal. I feel that a verbal contract is as good as a written one, but there are some artists who insist on a written contract. Whether you have a written agreement or a verbal one, these are some of the things that should be covered in the contract:

1. The amount of commission to be paid the gallery on sales made at the gallery and the amount of commission to be paid the gallery on sales made as a result of the gallery directing clients to the artist's studio.

53

2. The policy on transportation charges both to and from the gallery.

3. The policy on insurance coverage.

4. The length of time the gallery is to act as the artist's representative.

5. The length of time any given group of paintings shall remain in the gallery before they are to be returned and/or exchanged for other pieces.

6. The minimum and maximum number of pieces that are required for a show.

7. The minimum and maximum number of pieces that are expected to be at the gallery at times other than during a show.

8. A policy regarding exclusive rights. This should cover more than merely geographical exclusiveness. Let us assume that you have decided on geographical exclusiveness for a radius of one hundred miles. But, if within that one-hundred-mile radius there are ten galleries, you must establish a policy regarding those galleries. The artist should be willing to let you act as his agent for the galleries within this one-hundred-mile radius. In addition to this exclusive geographic area you must have an agreement regarding the different mediums with which the artist may work. If an artist works in oils, watercolors, lithos, and other mediums he should be willing to guarantee you exclusivity in all forms of his work. But spell this out clearly in your agreement.

9. The time and frequency of one-man shows. Cover the length of time a show will run and establish a tentative date if possible.

10. The responsibility of the artist and the responsibility of the gallery regarding expenses that arise at showtime. It may come as a surprise to you but it is a fact that many galleries expect the artist to pay a large portion, and at times the entire amount, of the expenses incurred during a show—invitations, brochures, mailing costs, advertising costs, and reception costs such as refreshments. The same thing applies here as with transportation costs. If the artist is not anxious to exhibit with your gallery at a one-man show but you are anxious to have him exhibit his work, then you may have to make the concessions. How many concessions are made will depend on the eagerness of the parties involved.

Till now we have been discussing the responsibility of expenses for a one-man show but the responsibility of expenses for a two/three-man show and group show should also be defined.

In a two/three man show it is a fair plan to equally divide the expenses between the participating artists, giving each artist equal billing on the invitations and brochures and equally publicity in the newspapers, radio and TV.

Where a group show is involved it is also a fair plan to divide the expenses between the participating artists, giving equal billing careful consideration.

11. Arrange to pay the artist on a monthly basis, with the understanding that no piece is considered sold until the client has paid for it in full.

12. The pieces presented for a show should be ready for exhibiting. Oils should be framed, even if simple slat framing is used. Prints should be either framed or nicely matted; if matted they should be protected with a cellophane or plastic covering. In addition, it should be understood that

pieces requiring special installation should be ready to install, complete with instructions. But if the installation is very complicated, the artist should come to the gallery and personally attend to whatever is necessary.

13. A policy regarding cancellations. A show should be cancelled only if both sides mutually agree. If any printing (invitations, brochures, etc.) has been completed, then the party instituting the cancellation procedure should be responsible for this expense.

Let me say that a contract is only as good as the word of the parties who enter into it. You are not likely to sue an artist if he does not fulfill his obligation to you, and an artist is not likely to sue your gallery. The worst that may happen is the termination of an agreement by mutual consent.

6

RECORD-KEEPING

Before going into the actual record-keeping, I would like to
suggest a list of abbreviations:

W/C = Watercolor	ACR = Acrylic
WD/C = Woodcut	ACR+O = Acrylic and Oil
ETCH = Etching	SCU = Sculpture
LITHO = Lithograph	CER = Ceramics
SS = Silkscreen	JEW = Jewelry
O = Oil	COL = Colored
MXM = Mixed Media	B/W = Black and White

These abbreviations will help facilitate your record-keeping,
as will a secret code that will provide a confidential recall of
the cost of each item. For example:

```
L E M O N   S Y R U P   or   B U I C K   S E D A N
1 2 3 4 5   6 7 8 9 0         1 2 3 4 5   6 7 8 9 0
```

If the cost of a piece is $100 less 40 percent or a net cost of $60, the code on the label would read either SP (using the LEMON SYRUP code) or SN (using the BUICK SEDAN code). Any phrase can be used for this secret code provided the phrase contains ten different letters.

Now let us proceed to some actual record-keeping.

ENTER ALL INCOMING PIECES

When you receive any piece of art, whether from an individual artist or from a wholesale representative, enter the piece or pieces on file cards. Give each piece a number using abbreviations to identify the type of piece, for example, W/C 1, W/C 2, WD/C 1, WD/C 2 (see Figures 1 and 2). Numbering is the logical means of reference to a work of art. Should you want to know how long any piece has been in the gallery you merely have to check its number on the artist's card and you have the date it was received.

Jot down the last number used for each category on a card and slip the card into a desk drawer. When you find it necessary to enter future incoming pieces, it will provide an up-to-date quick reference as to the last numbers used and furnish a point of reference for continuing the numbering where you left off.

DATE RECV'D	NO	DESCRIPTION				RETAIL PRICE	DATE SOLD	DATE PAID	DATE RETN'D

DISCOUNT 40%

ARDON Tom 72 REVERE RD ALLENTOWN PA   PHONE—

DATE RECV'D	NO	DESCRIPTION				RETAIL PRICE	DATE SOLD	DATE PAID	DATE RETN'D
2/1/70	W/C 10	SCENE IN ROCKPORT	UNFRAM.	10"x28"		45°°	6/3/70	7/1/70	
2/1/70	W/C 11	" "	"	"	"	45°°			7/1/70
2/1/70	W/C 12	SCENE IN SALEM	"	"	"	45°°	6/25/70	7/1/70	
9/15/70	W/C 64	FLORAL	"	"	"	55°°	3/16/71	4/1/71	
9/15/70	W/C 65	FLORAL	"	"	"	55°°	5/4/71	6/1/71	
9/15/70	W/C 66	SANDPIPERS	"	20"x28"		110°°	9/10/71	10/1/71	

Figure 1. Artist's card; 4 x 6 inches.

LABEL ALL PIECES

Mark the following information on a label: artist's name,
number, cost (in code), subject, and retail selling price. The
label should look like the following:

Tom Allen
W/C 101—EY
Scene in Rockport
$45.

59

			DISCOUNT 50%		
DANVERS JOHN G & Co INC 11 MAIN St. WATERTOWN MASS 617-123-4567					
DATE RECVD	NO	ARTISTS NAME	DESCRIPTION	RETAIL PRICE	DATE SOLD
1/16/70	LITHO 101	ENGEL	DAVID & BATSHEVA Col. 9"×12"	25 00	
1/16/70	LITHO 102	NISSON	DON QUIXOTE " " "	25 00	2/10/70
1/16/70	LITHO 103	LOUISE	CITY LIGHTS " 10"×20"	30 00	
1/16/70	ETCH 76	ALBEN	HEAD OF TIGER B/W 9"×12"	25 00	3/21/70
1/16/70	SS 35	NANA	PUSSY CAT Col 10"×16"	40 00	
1/16/70	W/C 86	LANDRY	ABSTRACT B/W 20"×28"	75 00	3/15/70
1/16/70	W/C 87	LANDRY	PRISONER B/W 20×28	75 00	2/1/70

Figure 2. Wholesaler's card; 4 x 6 inches.

Attach the label to the work of art, making certain not to cause any damage to a piece as a result of a stick-on label. And, of course, never place a label directly on a painting regardless of the medium. It is usually safe to place the label directly on the frame except when the frame is gold-leaf; a gummed label will cause the gold-leaf to peel when the label is removed. On a matted piece it is best to place the label either on the back of the mat or on the very corner of the front of the mat. With jewelry it is best to use a small string tag, and with ceramics and sculpture you won't usually have a problem finding a place for the label.

No. **9340** Dept._____ Date. 1/8 19 70

Name. *Mr. & Mrs. K. L. Smith*   445-2604

Address. *114 Walnut Terr. Syracuse 13214*

SOLD BY	CASH	C. O. D.	CHARGE	ON ACCT.	MDSE. RETD.	PAID OUT	
BW			X				

QUAN.		DESCRIPTION	PRICE	AMOUNT	
1	1	*016 Heavy Impasto*			
	2	*Artist Mc Claline*			
	3				
	4	*"Boating Scene in Maine"*	*210*	*00*	
	5				
	6	*7% Sales Tax*	*14*	*70*	
	7				
	8				
	9		*224*	*70*	
	10				
	11				
	12				
	13	WOLKIN GALLERY			
	14	100 MANOR DRIVE			
	15	SYRACUSE, N. Y. 13214			
	16				
	17				
	18				

Customer's Order No.		Rec'd By	*BW*	

Rediform **KEEP THIS SLIP FOR REFERENCE**

5H 33

Figure 3. Sales slip for charge.

RECORDING SALES

1. When you sell a piece make a sales slip in duplicate—(see Figure 3—client has charged the purchase on this transaction—and Figure 4—client has paid in full on this transac-

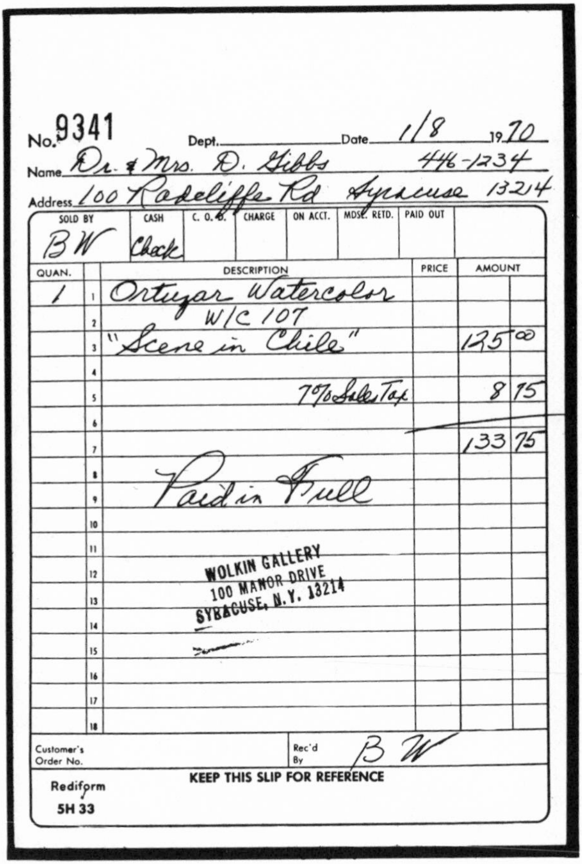

Figure 4. Paid sales slip.

tion). Give one sales slip to the customer and retain the other for your records.

At the end of each day bring your records up to date as follows:

2. Post every sales slip on a *Daily Sales Sheet* (see Figure 5). Total the *Daily Sales Sheet* and prepare for the next day's sales.

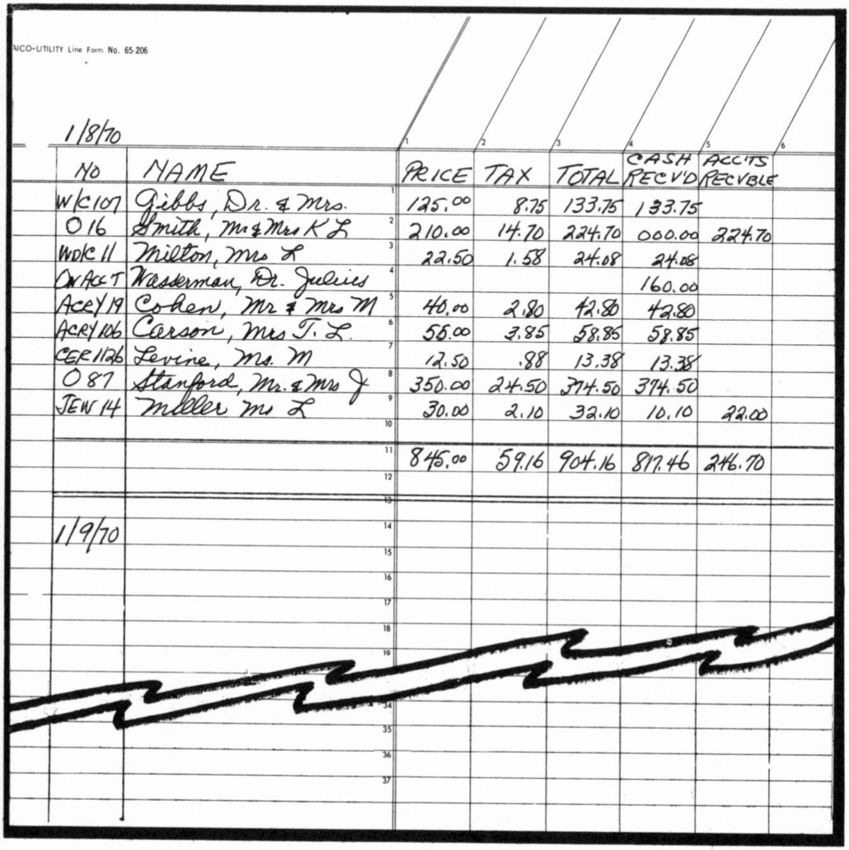

| NCO-UTILITY Line Form No. 65-206 | | | | | | |

1/8/70

NO	NAME	PRICE	TAX	TOTAL	CASH RECV'D	ACCT'S RECVBLE
WKC107	Gibbs, Dr. & Mrs.	125.00	8.75	133.75	133.75	
O16	Smith, Mr & Mrs K L	210.00	14.70	224.70	000.00	224.70
WDK11	Milton, Mrs L	22.50	1.58	24.08	24.08	
ON ACCT	Wasserman, Dr. Julius				160.00	
ACRY19	Cohen, Mr & Mrs M	40.00	2.80	42.80	42.80	
ACRY106	Carson, Mrs T. L.	55.00	3.85	58.85	58.85	
CER1126	Levine, Mr. M	12.50	.88	13.38	13.38	
O87	Stanford, Mr. & Mrs J	350.00	24.50	374.50	374.50	
JEW14	Miller, Mr L	30.00	2.10	32.10	10.10	22.00
		845.00	59.16	904.16	817.46	246.70

1/9/70

Figure 5. Daily sales sheet; 8½ x 11 inches.

DATE	No	ARTIST	DESCRIPTION	PRICE	DATE PAID

GIBBS DANIEL, DR (HELEN)   446-1234
100 RADCLIFFE RD   SYRACUSE N.Y. 13214
OFFICE: MEDICAL TOWERS   472-9025

DATE	No	ARTIST	DESCRIPTION	PRICE	DATE PAID
1/8/70	W/C 107	ORTUZAR	SCENE IN CHILE	125⁰⁰	1/8/70
4/6/71	W/C 32	SIEGL	TIPTOE (MATTED)	30⁰⁰	4/6/71
4/6/71	O 116	RON	JERUSALEM	300⁰⁰	4/6/71

Figure 6. Client's sales record card for charge; 4 x 6 inches.

3. Make a *Client's Sales Record* card for each new client (I use 4" x 6" cards). Make a card whether the client has paid for or charged the purchase (see Figures 6 and 7). File cards in a metal file box.

4. In addition to the *Client's Sales Record* card, a separate record should be made when the client buys a piece of art and charges the entire amount or pays a deposit and charges a balance. An *Accounts Receivable* should be recorded on this type of transaction (see Figure 8). (You can use a back portion of your Daily Sales notebook as your Accounts Receivable section.)

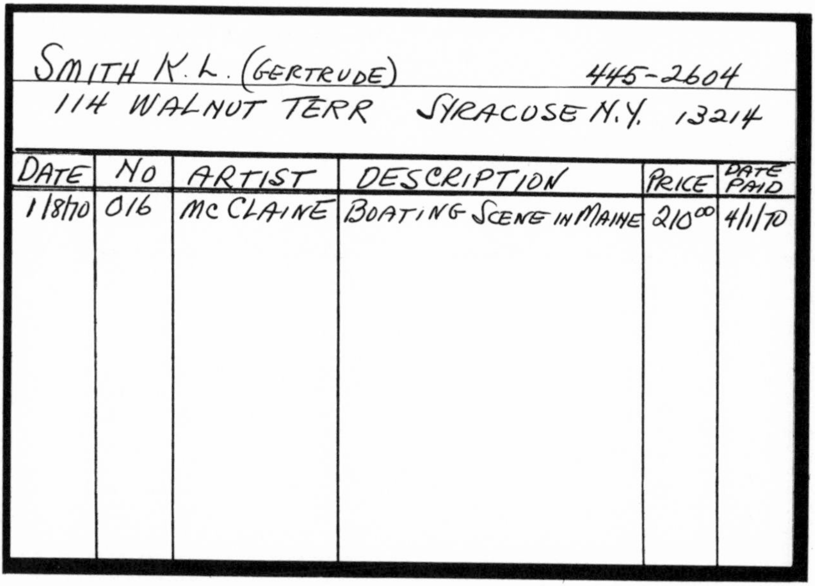

SMITH K. L. (GERTRUDE) 445-2604
114 WALNUT TERR SYRACUSE N.Y. 13214

DATE	NO	ARTIST	DESCRIPTION	PRICE	DATE PAID
1/8/70	016	MC CLAINE	BOATING SCENE IN MAINE	210.00	4/1/70

Figure 7. Client's sales record card; 4 x 6 inches.

In the case of a "charge" transaction, no date should be marked in the *"Date Paid"* column on the *Client's Sales Record* card until the unpaid balance has been paid in full (on Figure 7, note that sale was made January 8 and paid in full April 1).

Installment buying has become a way of life, and you will have many clients who buy in this manner. It is very important that you get some credit reference, even if only the client's bank, when he wants to charge any purchase over $100. You should also ascertain how long the client expects to take to pay the balance. Once a customer has established a good credit rating with you, you can then decide how much you are willing to allow him to charge to his account at any one time.

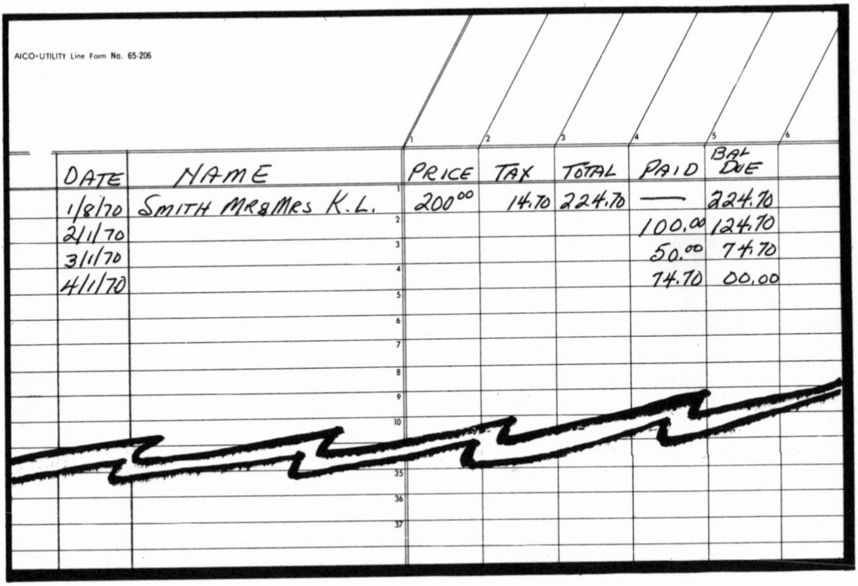

AICO-UTILITY Line Form No. 65-206

DATE	NAME	PRICE	TAX	TOTAL	PAID	BAL DUE
1/8/70	SMITH MR & MRS K.L.	200.00	14.70	224.70	—	224.70
2/1/70					100.00	124.70
3/1/70					50.00	74.70
4/1/70					74.70	00.00

Figure 8. Accounts receivable sheet; 8½ x 11 inches.

5. If you receive a check from a client as either full payment or partial payment on his account, give the client a receipt (see Figure 9). Post the amount paid on the *Daily Sales Sheet* (Figure 5) and post it on the client's *Accounts Receivable Sheet* (Figure 8).

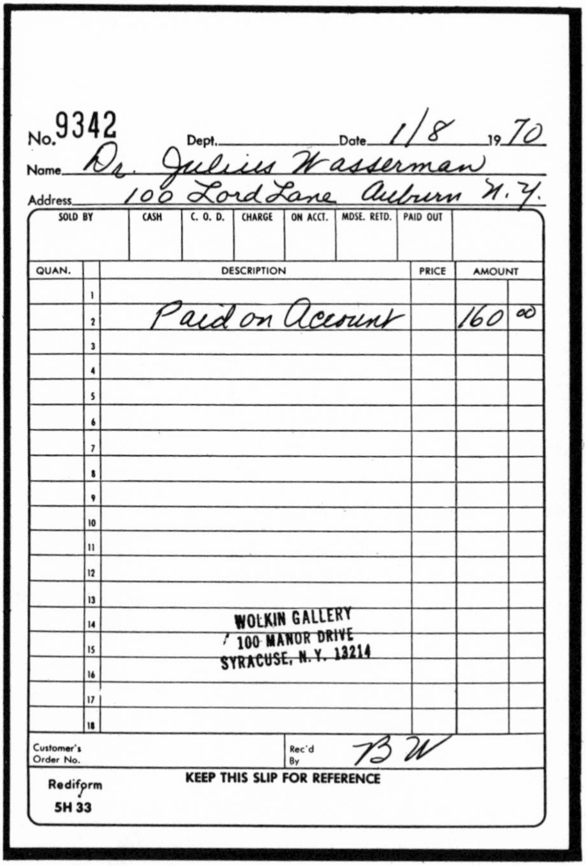

No. 9342 Dept._____ Date 1/8 19 70

Name Dr. Julius Wasserman

Address 100 Lord Lane Auburn N.Y.

SOLD BY	CASH	C. O. D.	CHARGE	ON ACCT.	MDSE. RETD.	PAID OUT	

QUAN.		DESCRIPTION	PRICE	AMOUNT	
	1				
	2	Paid on Account		160	00
	3				
	4				
	5				
	6				
	7				
	8				
	9				
	10				
	11				
	12				
	13				
	14	WOLKIN GALLERY			
	15	100 MANOR DRIVE			
	16	SYRACUSE, N.Y. 13214			
	17				
	18				

Customer's Order No. Rec'd By BW

Rediform 5H 33

KEEP THIS SLIP FOR REFERENCE

Figure 9. Receipt for money received on account.

6. Deduct the pieces sold from the artist's cards (Figure 1) and from the wholesale representative's card (Figure 2).

This automatically provides you with an accurate up-to-date daily inventory of the pieces in the gallery besides an accurate record of incoming pieces.

7. Go through procedures 1 through 6 for every sale and then file the duplicate sales slips either chronologically, according to date, or alphabetically according to the client's last name.

8. On the first of each month pay all your bills; not only monies due the artists, but also rent, freight, electricity, etc.

    The best procedure for paying your artists is to go through each artist's card and note what you marked "sold" (step No. 6). Send the artist a check for the pieces sold and record this on his/her card under the column marked "date paid" (Figure 1).

9. On the first of each month total all sales for the previous month. Take these figures from the *Daily Sales Sheets* (Figure 5) in order to arrive at the total. I use only the figures in the first column. My totals for the month do not reflect the sales tax. Record the monthly totals (see Figure 10).

    If you desire you can refine the monthly totals by breaking them down as to the type of pieces sold (see Figure 11):

    Paintings (all mediums). . . . .$575.
    Prints (WD/C-Litho-Etch-etc.,). . . . .$408.
    Ceramics . . . .$225.

Figures 10 and 11 are very important records. They enable you to compare monthly and yearly sales figures at a glance.

Do not fail to record the sales figures on shows and auctions done outside the gallery. These should be reflected in the monthly sales, which automatically will reflect them in the yearly figures.

A monthly record of expenditures and a record by month and year of these expenditures can prove valuable. You can determine just where your money has been spent by glancing at the overall picture this record paints. Incidentally, your check book and petty cash slips can be a big help when you record these items (see Figures 12 and 13).

It will be necessary to keep a journal when traveling on behalf of the gallery. It substantiates all your expenditures. Keep accurate account of every cent you spend (see Figure 14). This record, among others, will be needed when filing your income tax returns.

Speaking of income tax returns, I have always been inclined to leave this to a good accountant. A good accountant will earn his fee. There are deductions that are allowed by the IRS that the ordinary layman is not aware of; therefore, the amount an accountant will charge you will usually be compensated for by the amount he will save you. Nevertheless, establish the amount of the fee before you retain him or her.

		1970	1971	1972	1973
1	JANUARY	1634 25			
2	FEBRUARY	2862 10			
3	MARCH	3546 05			
4	APRIL	2111 10			
5	MAY	1006 00			
6	JUNE	643 00			
7	JULY	627 50			
8	AUGUST	403 00			
9	SEPTEMBER	3456 05			
10	OCTOBER	5866 25			
11	NOVEMBER	6743 05			
12	DECEMBER	9184 60			
13		37728 95			
14					
15					

		1981	1982	1983	
17					
19	JANUARY				
20	FEBRUARY				
21	MARCH				
22	APRIL				
23	MAY				
24	JUNE				
25	JULY				
26	AUGUST				
27	SEPTEMBER				
28	OCTOBER				
29	NOVEMBER				
30	DECEMBER				

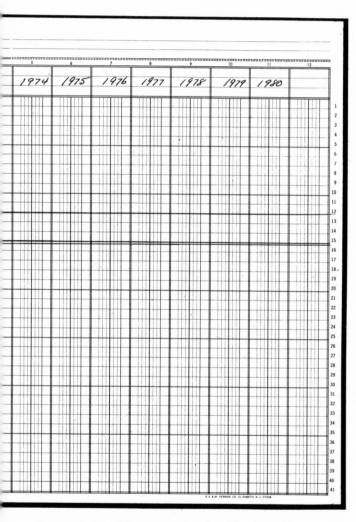

Figure 10. Monthly and yearly sales; 11 x 16 inches.

	Prepared By	Approved By
Initials		
Date		

	1. PAINTINGS ALL MEDIUMS	2. PRINTS w/o-LITHO ETC-ETC	3. CERAMICS	4. SCULPTURE
1970				
JANUARY	575 00	408 00	135 25	200 00
FEBRUARY	1050 00	575 00	950 10	200 00
MARCH	1175 00	1250 00	875 05	
APRIL	350 00	1275 00	486 10	
MAY	560 00	150 00	146 00	
JUNE	250 00	175 00	88 00	130 00
JULY		325 00	302 50	
AUGUST	200 00	100 00	103 00	
SEPTEMBER	1275 00	760 00	907 05	600 00
OCTOBER	2900 00	875 25	1500 00	500 00
NOVEMBER	2000 00	2250 00	2253 05	
DECEMBER	2850 00	2785 00	2787 60	1630 00
	13185 00	10928 25	10858 70	1630 00
1971				
JANUARY				
FEBRUARY				
MARCH				
APRIL				
MAY				
JUNE				
JULY				
AUGUST				
SEPTEMBER				
OCTOBER				
NOVEMBER				
DECEMBER				

NO 58-3402 GREEN-TINT NO 58-3412 BUFF RITE-ACROSS® MADE IN U.S.A.

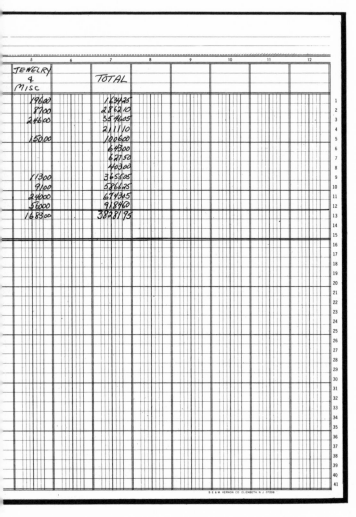

Figure 11. Monthly and yearly sales broken down; 11 x 16 inches.

DATE 1970	DESCRIPTION	CHECK No.	INVENTORY ART CRAFT ETC	GALLERY SUPPLIES	ADVERTISING PRINTING	FREIGHT AND MAILING
JAN 2	M. YOUNG	73				
2	NIAGARA MOHAWK	74				
2	TOM ARDON	75	240 00			
2	LUBLIN	76	180 00			
2	SANDMAN	77	86 00			
2	WOLF	78	300 00			
11	SHAYS - BOXES	79		9 30		
12	TRAFFIC TICKET	80				
15	GARNET NEWSPAPER	81			34 03	
15	SHOPPING NEWS	82			37 44	
16	JEWISH LEDGER	83			15 00	
15	STAMPS	84				2 40
15	N.Y. TELEPHONE	85				
15	MARY BELL	86				
16	HALL PRESS (INVITATIONS)	87			130 00	
	(+BROCHURES)					
21	BW SEE DIARY	88				
21	5LB COFFEE	89		4 75		
21	LIQUOR SQUARE SOUTH	90		15 00		
21	SWEET SHOP	91		4 00		
28	REA EXPRESS	92				9 34
30	MISC - PETTY CASH					
			806 00	33 05	216 47	11 74

NO. 58-2412 GREEN-TINT   NO. 58-2812 BUFF   RITE ACROSS®   MADE IN U.S.A.

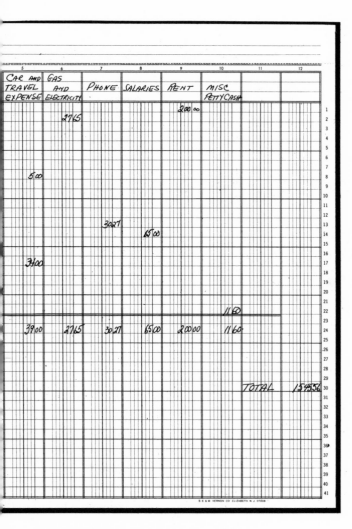

Figure 12. Monthly expenses; 11 x 16 inches.

				Initials	Date
			Prepared By		
			Approved By		

			1	2	3	4
YEAR	MONTH		INVENTORY ART CRAFT ETC	GALLERY SUPPLIES	ADVERTISING AND PRINTING	FREIGHT AND MAILING
1970						
1	JANUARY		806.00	33.05	216.47	117.56
2	FEBRUARY		1509.56	85.00	285.00	6.52
3	MARCH		3106.50	117.60	375.00	226.5?
4	APRIL		197.25	60.56	195.00	42.00
5	MAY		1625.50	49.25	171.47	56.86
6	JUNE					
7	JULY					
8	AUGUST					
9	SEPTEMBER					
10	OCTOBER					
11	NOVEMBER					
12	DECEMBER					
13						
14						
15						
16						
17						
18	1971	JANUARY				
19		FEBRUARY				
20		MARCH				
21		APRIL				
22		MAY				
23		JUNE				
24		JULY				
25		AUGUST				
26		SEPTEMBER				
27		OCTOBER				
28		NOVEMBER				
29		DECEMBER				
30						
31						
32						
33						
34						
35						
36						
37						
38						
39						
40						
41						

NO. 58-2412 GREEN-TINT NO. 58-2412 BUFF RITE-ACROSS® MADE IN U.S.A.

CAR AND TRAVEL EXPENSE	GAS AND ELECTRICITY	PHONE	SALARIES	RENT	MISC PETTY CASH	TOTAL	
39 00	26 75	30 77	65 00	200 00	11 60	1546 36	1
20 00	34 28	22 17	120 00	200 00		234 28	2
22 00	32 26	44 10	120 00	200 00	8 50	424 51	3
37 60	21 08	29 66	105 00	200 00	6 75	874 89	4
13 00	11 25	28 07	85 00	200 00		224 40	5

Figure 13. Monthly and yearly expenses; 11 x 16 inches.

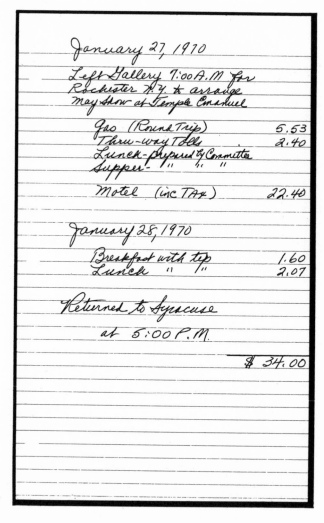

Figure 14. List of expenditures when traveling.

It is a good idea to take inventory every six months. The inventory should correspond with what is reflected on your artist's cards (Figure 1) and wholesaler's cards (Figure 2). You can determine if there has been any pilfering and, if so, tighten up your security. Inventory time is also a time to evaluate your sales. What has sold well and what has sold poorly? Inventory time is an especially good time to evaluate your pottery and ceramic sales:

Number of mugs sold
Number of tea sets sold
Number of casseroles sold
Number of sculptured pieces sold
etc., etc., etc.,

Such evaluations can be excellent guides to future ordering.

Record-keeping can be very simple and take very little time if you do not allow it to accumulate. Make it a daily habit. You will find it pays off in the long run.

7

PUBLICITY

NEWSPAPERS

Unless money is of no consequence, you will probably have to be your own publicist or press agent, because it is extremely costly to hire one. Most artists will supply you with well-written biographies and press releases. If they do not, let me give you a few guidelines that I have found helpful:

1. Use a straightforward approach when writing about the artist's training and background. Include date and place of birth.

2. Include past shows, awards, quotes from previous favorable reviews, and the names of collectors owning his work.

3. Describe the artist's work in a manner that makes his technique easy to visualize.

4. Refrain from using flowery exaggerations and ambiguities.

Make every attempt to get as much free publicity as you can. Send press releases, including a picture of one of the artist's pieces, to the women's section editor and to the art editor of your daily newspapers. There is usually a cultural calendar in the Sunday newspaper, and in most instances there is no charge for a listing in this section. This cultural calendar is a most effective vehicle for notifying readers of coming events. It is necessary to advise the editor of the cultural calendar when your shows change in order that your listing may be kept up to date.

Paid advertising should be placed in local newspapers and suburban "shopping guides." Try to determine the best day and the best section of the newspaper for your type of advertising. I have found the following schedule of advertising very effective: Place an ad in the Sunday newspaper on two consecutive Sundays before an opening and have an additional ad appear on the day of the opening. Newspaper ad salesmen are very helpful, so don't hesitate to consult them regarding your advertising.

Most newspapers have an incentive plan for their customers. They offer special rates to steady advertisers. This special rate may cost less than placing ads sporadically. Inquire about it and take advantage of the offer if there is a savings.

There are also FM radio stations that make spot announcements of cultural events at a very minimal cost, and these also are effective.

INVITATIONS AND BROCHURES

Find a good printer who can be helpful with invitations and brochures.

Invitations can vary from a simple postcard idea to a very detailed booklet complete with colored reproductions of the artist's work. It is important that your invitations have "class." They should attract attention! They should be creative! They should be appealing! A good printer can help you accomplish much of this through unusual printing techniques.

It is important that invitations be mailed out at the proper time—neither too soon nor too late. A good rule is to post your invitations ten days before the opening date of the show.

There are times when all the facts about an artist can be listed on the invitation in addition to the 4 W's (who, what, where, and when). In such cases a brochure is not necessary. However, when an artist has a long list of awards, collectors, and accomplishments, it is a good idea to have a brochure in addition to the invitation. The brochure should be available to the guests who come to the gallery for the show.

The status of the artist often dictates the type of invitation and brochure to be printed.

MAILING LIST

Until such time as you develop your own mailing list, it is a good idea to contact churches, synagogues, and community centers that might be willing to give you their membership lists. Many such groups will cooperate because they are happy to have their members notified of coming cultural events.

Now There Ar

By GRACE GLUECK

"Forget Polaroid and Motorola," an investor told his broker the other day. "I want a piece of that Picasso-Monet action."

He was slightly premature, but not misinformed. Spurred by soaring art prices over the last decade, a collision is taking place between art and Wall Street. To the dismay of collectors, critics and dealers, the average investor may soon be able to buy shares in art as easily as he buys corporate stocks.

At least three public art investment funds are being formed here, and there are reports of others. In Paris, a French-Dutch-Belgian fund is developing that hopes also for American backing and plans to buy American works of art as part of its inventory. In addition, several art gallery chains have gone or are going public.

All Need Approval

All of the funds await approval by the Securities and Exchange Commission, and only one has acquired any of the art inventory in which it proposes to sell shares. Two whose prospectuses are available for inspection are The Art Fund and the Sovereign-American Arts Corporation, which hope to sell respectively 1 million shares at $5 and 200,000 shares at $6. A third fund, as yet untitled, is said to be aiming for a $25-million public issue.

In general, the art funds' operation may be compared with that of mutual funds. They plan to buy selected works of art as mutual funds would buy selected securities, and hold on to them for capital gains. The art would be traded for profit as opportunities arose.

The public investment funds are different from private investment syndicates, a number of which are established throughout the country. In the latter, small groups of investors pool money on a more or less informal basis to buy works of art. One example is the John Adams Fund, Inc., a New York group that buys only blue-chip impressionist and post-impressionist works. It does not sell public shares.

In the case of The Art Fund, the plan is to assemble a collection "of museum quality and stature" and keep it in supervised storage, making items and groups of items available for loan to institutions. Sovereign-American also holds its art in storage, and may let stockholders hang some of it in their homes.

Though still in registration with the S.E.C., the funds have already drawn fire from the art world, on grounds ranging from esthetics to economics. With regard to the latter, experts say the widespread belief that "art is better than the stock market" has proved true only in the long haul—over decades—and then only in the case of certain names and categories. In the short, speculative run, they point out, investing in anything less than blue chip art is just as chancy as cocoa futures or pork bellies.

Idea Began in London

The first of the funds to get under way is Sovereign-American, hatched a year-and-a-half ago in London by a group of British and American investors. Its prime movers are Nicholas Guppy, a London-based bota-

nist, writer and exhib
organizer, who holds 9
shares, and two America
Richmond Lilse-Cannon
New York investor,
Nichols Kirkbride, until
cently director of a fir
newspaper representa
Each holds 5,000 shares.
other overseas principa
Lord Ulick Browne, an
peer, who owns 5,000 sh

Sovereign-American, w
buys "world art" over
last two centuries, has a
chief art advisers Sir
Rothenstein, ex-director
London's Tate Gallery,
Robert Beverly Hale, for
ly curator of American p
ings and sculpture at
Metropolitan Museum,
now on the Art Committ
the Chase Manhattan B
Each holds 1,000 share
the fund.

The . fund's prosp
lists over 70 works of art
it has acquired to date.
range is from such nam
Corot, Calder, Kandinsk
acometti and Moore to
tive unknowns such as
ser Assar, of whose worl
fund owns two examples

Adviser Leaves Fund

The Boston-based Art
was conceived by Mr. Po
and Michael Winer, a f
cial consultant, each of v
owns 2,500 shares. Unt
cently it had as its chie
adviser Sam Hunter, art
and historian, who is p
sor of art history at Pi
ton University. But
Hunter, who had an c
on 20,000 shares, and
listed as director of
fund's executive comm
withdrew last week
grounds that his particip
might represent a co
of interest with his aca
activities. Victor W

E NEW YORK TIMES, FRIDAY, NOVEMBER 7, 1969

Mutual Funds for Art

Figure 15. Art column by nationally syndicated columnist. Illustration of painting deleted. © *1969 by the New York Times Company. Reprinted by permission.*

ew York business man prominent collector, al-esigned as a director.

der guidelines laid down Mr. Hunter, the fund to collect in five cate-s: established contem-y Americans like Cal-Pollock and Rauschen-major examples of ern masters, like Picasso, linsky and Moore, late and early 20th-century rican masters, contem-ry Europeans, both es-shed and of more recent tation, and works by ising younger American s.

Artists Promised Aid

In its prospectus, the Art Fund says that "it will encourage the expansion of the world arts movement by focusing on the works of living artists." And it promises to apply a percentage of the gains from sales of work by living artists to a charitable foundation that will give grants to other artists.

Art world reaction to the fund proposals has generally been unfavorable. One corporation lawyer made the point that art was not as liquid as securities. "You can buy a Gauguin for, say, $100,000 — but it's not so easy to find a buyer for it when you want to sell it."

A typical comment on esthetic grounds was made by Mrs. Howard Lipman, a prominent collector of contemporary sculpture and editor of the magazine Art in America.

"To me, the concept of art investment is as bad as air pollution," she said. "It's dealing with art as a commodity, a total confusion of values."

The following institutions and people should automatically be on your mailing list: churches, synagogues, art schools (university and private), radio stations, TV stations, editors of newspapers (especially the women's editor and the art editor), curators and directors of museums, decorators, art associations (including craft clubs), libraries, community centers, and banks. Many such places have bulletin boards, and those in charge will gladly post your invitation if you include a handwritten note thanking them in advance for doing so.

There are times when national syndicated columnists write articles referring to art (see an example by Grace Glueck, Figure 15). Be on the alert for any article of this type, have it inexpensively reproduced, making certain of course to get reprint permission from the newspaper and/or the author, and include the reproduction in some of your mailings. You would do well to read pages 972 to 976 in *Sylvia Porter's Money Book* (Garden City, N. Y.: Doubleday, 1975). This information makes fine talking points for convincing any client of the advantages of owning original works of art.

One of the best forms of publicity is a satisfied client. Word-of-mouth, especially if it's favorable, can build your clientele very quickly.

It is also a very good idea to be listed in the yellow pages of your local telephone directory.

Figures 16 through 26 provide examples of invitations, brochures, ads, and press releases.

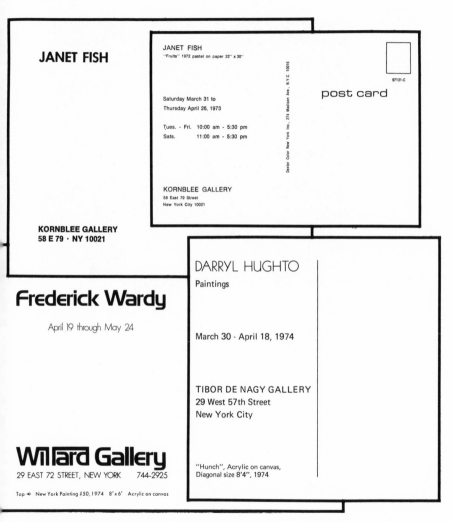

Figure 16. Exhibit notices backed by reproductions of artists' works; sizes vary from 4 x 6 inches to 5 x 7 inches.

Figure 17. Single-fold invitation with artist's biography and show announcement on inside; the artist's photo is carried on the cover; 5¾ x 9½ inches.

FAYETTEVILLE FRAMING AND THE WOLKIN GALLERY

515 E. GENESEE ST., FAYETTEVILLE, N. Y.

PRESENT A

ONE MAN EXHIBITION

OF THE

ISRAELI ARTIST

JOSEPH IJAKY

PREVIEW SHOWING WEDNESDAY, OCTOBER 9, 7 TO 9:30 P.M.

OPENING TO THE PUBLIC THURSDAY, OCTOBER 10TH, UNTIL OCTOBER 29TH

GALLERY HOURS: TUES. THRU SAT. 9:00-5:00
TUES. & WED. EVE 7-9 P.M.
BY APPOINTMENT — PHONE: 637-9001 OR 446-3474

Other Works of Art by
well known Israeli Artists

Mr. Ijaky was born in Transylvania in 1922 and as a child showed great promise with the brush and pallete.

He studied at the Academy of Arts in Budapest and privately with the best teachers in Bucharest and Paris, coming to Israel to live in 1960.

His works have been sent abroad and exhibited with glowing reports from the Critics. Milan — 1961. Paris and Geneva — 1963. Frankfurt — 1964. Munich — 1965. Brussels, Copenhagen, Montreal and New York — 1966. Currently Mr. Ijaky is traveling in Europe where he is exhibiting in London, Paris and Antwerp. He will arrive in the United States in December for his One Man show in New York City.

Gordon Muck, well known teacher, artist and art critic, has said of Ijaky, "Using polymer and pallete knife strokes, he captures the sun-baked evanescent quality of Israeli cities with rich but often subtle color. He paints with an impressionists pallete, strong linear framework and considerable spontaneity."

Figure 18. Single-fold invitation showing artist's biography on inside; the announcement and artist's photo are carried on the outside; 8½ x 11 inches.

HALL GROAT PAINTINGS

HOME:
Cazenovia, New York

STUDIED:
Syracuse University School of Art
Studied under Josef Albers of Yale University

ONE MAN SHOWS (partial list)

Berkshire Museum, Pittsfield, Mass.
Gallery Montage, Syracuse
New York Telephone Co., Syracuse
Jewish Community Center, Huntington, L.I.
Verzyl Gallery, Northport, L.I.
Eleanor Dennis Studio, Washington Mt., Mass.
Tyringham Gallery, Tyringham, Mass.
Associated Artists of Syracuse
Wellfleet Gallery, Palm Beach, Florida

EXHIBITIONS:
Associated Artists of Syracuse — 1960 award
Everson Museum
Rochester Memorial Gallery
Munson Proctor Museum
Berkshire Museum — 1962 purchase award
Buffalo, N.Y. Seventh Annual — 1963 award
Pittsfield Art League — 1962, 1965 awards
Cooperstown Art Association — 1964, 1965 honorable mentions; 1966, 1967
Springfield Expositions
New York State Fair — 1964 purchase award
Mystic, Conn. — 1965 award
Moorestown, N.J. — 1966 award
Butler Institute of American Art — 1967
Roberson Center of Arts & Sciences

COLLECTIONS:
Berkshire Museum
Syracuse University
State University at Morrisville
Kenneth Sargent
Frederick Webster
Thomas Crenshaw
Milo Folley
Dr. Herbert I. Katz
(Many private collections throughout the U.S. & Canada)

MURALS:
Republic of Korea (Naval)
Liverpool, N.Y. (Historical, 4 panels)
General Electric, Pittsfield, Mass. (Naval and Space Age, 2 panels)
Johnstown High School, Johnstown, N.Y. (Abstract, one of the largest
auditorium murals in the U.S., 2 walls.)

BABE SHAPIRO

Paintings: 1965-1975
November 1-20, 1975

ΛM SACHS

29 West 57 Street, New York, N.Y. 10019

NOVEMBER 4 - 26, 1975
BETTY PARSONS GALLERY   24 W. 57th ST., N.Y.C.

ELAINE DE KOONING

RECENT PAINTINGS

November 8 through November 29, 1975
Opening Saturday, November 8th, 1 p.m.- 5 p.m.

GRAHAM

1014 MADISON AVENUE, NEW YORK 10021   212-535-5767

Both exhibitions to
open October 25, 1-5 p.m.
through November 21

Alfred Leslie

Recent Paintings: 50 West 57th Street, New York
Recent Drawings: 41 East 57th Street, New York

ALLAN FRUMKIN GALLERY

Robert Ryman

Paintings and Prints
November 1 to 26 1975

John Weber Gallery   420 West Broadway N.Y.

Figure 19. Postcard announcements of shows, backed by address space.

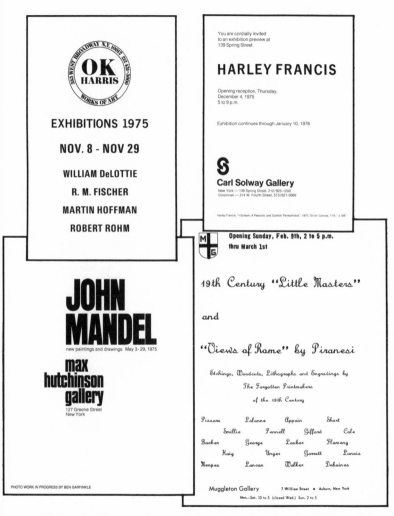

Figure 20. Exhibit notices varying in size from 5 x 7 inches to 6 x 9 inches.

Studied at Carnegie Tech, School of Fine Arts, and the Art Students League with Edwin Dickenson, Frank Reilly, Ivan Olinsky, Robert Hale and Howard Trafton. Studied the art of stone lithography at the Pratt Center for Contemporary Graphics.

Grew up in Israel as a boy, and subsequently returned there on completing studies at the Art Students League of N.Y. Taught art and painted in Israel.

Actively associated in art for many leading Israeli and Jewish organizations.

A constant student whose work reflects continued gentleness and love of positiveness of life.

Has won many awards in painting and graphics.

Widely exhibited in many galleries and private collections throughout the United States (Brooklyn Museum, Nassau Community College, City Hall, N.Y., Newark State College). Exhibited in Israel in galleries and in many private collections including the permanent collections of The Museum of Israel (Jerusalem); The Museum of Haifa; The Building of the Chief Rabbinate, Jerusalem; The Mayor of Jerusalem's private collection; Bar Ilan University in Ramat Gan; Tel Aviv University; Hebrew University, Jerusalem; Int'l Synagogue, N.Y.

In the permanent collection of The Jewish Museum, N.Y.; The Brooklyn Museum; Kansas City Art Institute.

Listed in Who's Who in American Art and Who's Who in the International Directory of Art.

536 Kirkby Road/Elmont, Long Island, N.Y. 11003
(516) 354-0448

Definition of an Original Print

"Each print, in order to be considered an original, must bear not only the signature of the artist, but also an indication of total edition and the serial number of the print. Prints pulled by the artist to show progress (artist's proof-limited usually to ten percent of the total edition or 1st state or 2nd state trial proofs) should not be included in total number of print edition."

From definition of an Original Print agreed at the Third International Congress of Artists, Vienna, Sept. 1960

Prints which may not be classed as original prints:

Copies of original works of art made wholly by photo-mechanical or other mechanical processes even tho' they may be in limited editions, and bear the signature of the artist whose work is reproduced.

The Artist should be the one who draws the image directly onto his plate, and not have it done by photomechanical methods, as certain prints done by offset lithography or in silk-screen prints. These prints have no value, monetarily or artistically.

SUNDAY ☀ NEWS
NEW YORK'S PICTURE NEWSPAPER®

Elmont Artist Is Master of Ancient Form

To make a stone lithograph print, Schary must first draw his sketch with grease pencil on a porous stone found only in a small town in Bavaria.

The stone is then etched with an acid solution. When ink is applied to the stone, the acid and water repel the ink, while the grease retains it.

Working with one of the few master printers in the U.S., capable of such work, the artist applies a slightly dampened paper to the stone. The paper, handcrafted in France, is designed to last a lifetime.

The printer rolls the heavy stone, which is a minimum of three inches thick, through a mangle press under tremendous pressure.

Provided the artist or the printer didn't goof during any of the delicate steps, a print of amazing clarity results with incredible, subtle shades.

The printer, if all goes well, should be able to produce about 250 prints of equal quality before the chemical composition breaks down.

Schary's work, which reveals a realistic and delicate beauty, has earned him a listing in Who's Who in the International Directory of Art.

His lithographs sell for about $60 each while his works in oil can't be had for less than $500.

Schary's process is not to be confused with etchings made on metal plates, which are common, can be produced quickly and do not require unerring control during the printing process.

"Stone lithography is a medium where you can't afford to make mistakes," Schary said. "Many of today's artists are interested in instant results. I'm willing to work extra hard for excellence."

In today's competitive art world where flashy fads and intellectual put-ons can catapult an artist into an overnight success, an introspective Long Island artist has stirred a new and growing interest in the dying art of stone lithography.

The artist, Emanuel Schary of Elmont, is one of the few painters left in the world working mostly in that ancient and laborious medium. As a result, he widely exhibited in galleries throughout the country, including the Brooklyn Museum, Nassau Community College and New York's City Hall.

Unlike many contemporary artists who mirror the strident forces affecting our war-plagued and pollution-periled planet, Schary portrays the "positiveness of life" and concentrates on Hebraic themes.

Working at his home in 536 Kirkby Rd., he has produced and sold many thousands of works, including commissioned paintings and limited editions in the past few years.

Michael Patterson

Figure 21. Brochure providing artist's biography; 8½ x 11 inches.

DAVID BUMBECK

Born Framingham, Massachusetts, 1940.

B.F.A., Rhode Island School of Design, 1962.
    Annual Rhode Island Scholar Award.
    European Honors Program.
    Represented school at Annual Banquet of Rhode Island Colleges, 1961.

Art Supervisor, Lebanon, New York, Central Schools, 1963-64.

M.F.A., Syracuse University, 1966.
    Full scholarship, Graduate Assistant in Drawing and Design.

Instructor of Painting, Printmaking, and Drawing, Massachusetts College of Art, 1966-68.

Assistant Professor of Printmaking, Design, and Drawing, Middlebury College, 1968-present.

Married, has two children.

Group Exhibitions:
    Providence, Rhode Island, Annual Drawing Show, First Prize, 1961.
    Oklahoma National Print Exhibition, 1966.
    Hartford Atheneum National Exhibition, 1966.
    Munson-Williams-Proctor Institute Regional Exhibition, 1966.
    Everson Museum Regional Exhibition, Purchase Award for Painting, 1966.
    Fingerlakes Regional Exhibition, 1966.
    Rhode Island Art Festival, 1967.
    Nazareth College National Print Exhibition, 1968.
    Newport Art Festival, 1968.
    Waterbury Art Festival, First Prize in Graphics, 1968.
    "Graphics 69" National Print Exhibition, New York State Fair, 1969.
    Georgia State University National Print Exhibition, Purchase Award, 1970.
    Northern Illinois University National Print Exhibition, 1970.
    Boston Printmakers National Exhibition, Museum of Fine Arts, Boston, 1967, 1968, 1969, 1970.
        David Berger Memorial Award, 1968.   Elected to Executive Board of Boston Printmakers.

One Man Shows:
    George Walter Vincent Smith Museum, 1966.   Lyman Allyn Museum, 1969.
    Emma Willard School, 1968.   Ithaca Museum, 1969.
    Berkshire Museum, 1968.   University of Georgia, 1969.
    S.U.N.Y. College at Cortland, 1968.   Vermont College, 1970.
    Middlebury College, 1968.

Collections:
    National Mint Museum.   Middlebury College.
    Cortland State College.   Syracuse University.
    Vermont College.   Rochester Memorial Galleries.
    University of Colorado.   Ithaca Museum.
    Everson Museum.   Fitchburg Museum.
    New York Public Library Print Room.   Slater Memorial Museum.
    De Cordova Museum.   Georgia State University.

Figure 22. Artist's biography for distribution at a show; 8½ x 11 inches.

INVEST IN ART? WHY NOT?

ORIGINAL PRINTS UP 100%-150%

See our portfolio of prints by Picasso, Miro, Chagall, Rembrandt and others.

MUGGLETON GALLERY   7 William St. Auburn, N.Y.

Mon.-Sat. 10-5 (Closed Wednesdays)
By appointment phone 252-4433

Closed Today

Opening Sun., 4/21/74
"Gardens of Eden"

Recent prints by

Harold Altman

Muggleton Gallery

7 William St., Auburn
(Closed Wed.)

**TODAY 2-5
FINAL WEEK**

"An outstanding collection of original prints and handcrafted jewelry is on display at the Muggleton Gallery in Auburn through April 6.

Here are prints to please every taste. Many are important enough to be good investments in these days of galloping inflation — or simply prestigious additions to a modest collection. For the beginning collector, the entire exhibtion offers an opportunity to study the great variety of media and techniques used in printmaking."

By ANN HARTRANFT

Muggleton Gallery

7 Williams St., Auburn
(CLOSED WED.)

POTTERY BY...

LORRAINE HOGGS

OPENING TODAY 2 TO 5

THROUGH APRIL 19
ASSOCIATED ARTISTS
200 HIGH BRIDGE ST.,
FAYETTEVILLE
TUES.-SAT. 11-4; SUN. 2-5

U-FRAME-IT
Do it yourself
picture framing
• **SAVE MONEY** •
Hours: Mon.-Sat. 9 to 6
Mon. or Thur. eve. by appt.
**ARTISTS WORKSHOP
GALLERY & FRAMERS**
407 Oak St. (off James St.)
phone: 476-5088

Figure 23. Examples of newspaper advertising.

The Muggleton Gallery

offers . . . .

Oil Paintings
Watercolors
Signed Prints
Sculpture

Handcrafted:
Ceramics
Glass
Pewter
Jewelry

and

custom framing from the largest
selection of picture mouldings
in Central New York.

Muggleton
Gallery

7 William Street
Auburn, N.Y.
Phone 252-4433

Figure 24.
Double-fold gallery
promotion brochure;
8½ x 11 inches.

The Muggleton Gallery is located in downtown Auburn in one of the oldest homes in the city. The house was built in the 1820's and has been recently renovated. Eight rooms, completely furnished, are used for the display of art objects. Works by contemporary artists, as well as those of the 19th century, are artistically displayed in the various rooms.

Paintings and sculpture as displayed in one of the first floor show rooms of this early 19th century "house gallery".

In the display rooms on the second floor there are original prints by Picasso, Miro, Chagall, Friedlaender, Calder, Kollwitz and Levine, along with several paintings and sculpture pieces by recognized contemporary artists.

"Auburn is fortunate in being blessed with a gallery that concentrates on fine work by leading artists showing a wide range of stylistic trends and prices. It should be a great asset to the collector in Central New York."

Gordon F. Mack, Art Critic for
Syracuse Post Standard

Contemporary works by Baskin and Marx are shown hanging over the fireplace in the Gallery Room. Paintings and drawings by several New York State artists are to be found on display in this room. Many pottery and ceramic pieces are also arranged in this display.

"The Muggleton Gallery has a gracious and comfortable atmosphere where high quality art and crafts are selected with discrimination and displayed with taste."

Ann Hartranft, Art Critic for
Syracuse Herald Journal

What is an original print?

An "original print" is the image on paper or similar material made by one or more of the processes described here. Each medium has a special, identifiable quality but because more than one impression of each image is possible, "Original" does not mean "unique."

The artist's intention to create an original print is the key to the "originality" of the finished work. For example, if he first conceives of a watercolor, then has the result copied by woodcut, the result is not "original" but merely a reproduction. The total number of prints made of one image is an "edition." The number may appear on the print with the individual print number as a fraction such as 5/25 meaning "edition" was 25 examples with this example numbered 5. If intended for use with a written text original prints will not likely be numbered (or hand-signed) and may be produced in very large editions.

COLOR: Blocks, plates, screens or two or more stones may be used, one for each color, printed on top of each other to produce the final print.

RESTRIKES AND CANCELLED PLATE PROOFS: Both are original prints but from unlimited editions usually printed after an artist's death.

Original Graphic Arts Processes:

PROCESS:	RELIEF	INTAGLIO	PLANOGRAPHIC	STENCIL
Common Name:	(A) Woodcut / Linocut / Embossing (B) Wood Engraving COLLOGRAPH	Engraving / Drypoint / Mezzotint / Etching / Aquatint	Lithograph	Serigraph (Silkscreen)
What area prints:	Prints what is left of the original surface	Prints what is below the surface of the plate	Prints what is drawn on the surface	Prints open areas of the stencil. Original Serigraphs are usually hand screened
Type of Press:	(A) Household tablespoon (B) Washington Press or Letterpress	Etching Press (Clotheswringer type)	Litho Press (Sliding, scraping pressure)	
Materials:	(A) Plank-grain wood / Linoleum (B) End-grain wood	Copper / Zinc / Plastics, etc.	Limestone / Aluminum Plates, etc.	Silk / Organdie / Nylon, etc.
Basic Tools:	Knife / Gouge / Burin, etc.	Etching Needles / Burins / Acids / Grounds, etc.	Litho Crayon / Tusche / Litho Rubbing ink, etc.	Squeegee / Screen / Nufilm / Glue / Tusche, etc.

wood, usually with a knife. (The linocut is made by the same method, except that linoleum is substituted for wood.) In working the block, the artist cuts away areas not meant to print. These cut away areas appear in the finished print as the white parts of the design while the ink adheres to the raised parts.

WOOD-ENGRAVING: Made by engraving a block made up of pieces of end-grain, extremely hard wood. The block, being naturally much harder, enables the artist to engrave (rather than cut) a much finer line than is possible on the softer plank surface used for woodcuts.

COLLOGRAPH: Printing surface is built up on the plate or block by applying various materials which may also be incised.

ETCHING: A metal plate is coated by a material which resists acid, called the ground. The artist then draws his design on the ground with a sharp needle which removes the ground where it touches it and, when the plate is put in an acid bath, these exposed parts will be etched (or eaten away). This produces the sunken line which will receive the ink. In printing, the ink settles in the sunken areas and the plate is wiped clean. The plate in contact with damp paper is passed through a roller press and the paper is forced into the sunken area to receive the ink. The artist etches a plate those parts which will appear in the finished print as black or colored areas. White areas are left untouched. Depth of tone is controlled by depth of etch.

with a burin, then the plate is printed as above.

DRYPOINT: The sunken lines are produced directly by diamond-hard tools pulled across the plate. The depth of line is controlled by the artist's muscle and experience. The method of cutting produces a ridge along the incisions, called burr. This gives the dry-point line the characteristically soft, velvety appearance absent in the clean-edged lines of an engraving or etching.

AQUATINT: A Copper plate is protected by a porous ground which is semi-acid resistant. The white (non-printing) areas, however, are painted with a wholly acid-resistant varnish. The plate is then repeatedly put in acid baths where it is etched to differing depths. The final effect is an image on a fine pebbled background (imparted by the porous ground). Aquatint is usually employed in combination with line etching.

LITHOGRAPH: The artist draws directly on a flat stone or specially prepared metal plate (usually with a greasy crayon). The stone is dampened with water, then inked. The ink clings to the greasy crayon marks but not to the dampened areas. When a piece of paper is pressed against the stone, the ink on the greasy parts is transferred to it.

SERIGRAPH: The artist prepares a tightly-stretched screen, usually of silk, and blocks out areas not to be printed by filling those parts of the screen with a varnish-like substance. Paper is placed under the screen and ink forced through the still-open mesh onto the paper.

Buying original prints

If you have $100,000 you can buy an original Picasso. If you have $5000 you can buy an original Picasso. If you have $500 you can buy an original Picasso. You can buy an original Picasso for $50.

How? Well, for $100,000 you can buy an original oil painting. For $5000 an original drawing. For $500 an original graphic work (etching, lithograph, woodcut, or linoleum cut) signed by the artist and in a limited edition. For $50 or even less an original graphic work by Picasso, unsigned and unlimited but nevertheless an original.

Art appreciation increases with understanding. You might want to begin your collection with works signed by major artists whose works are known to you. The more you can learn about art, about original prints, about the works of a school or a single artist — the more you will enjoy collecting. Buy from reputable dealers (your local art museum or art center may be able to make recommendations). Fine art is generally considered a reasonable investment, and original graphic works are no exception.

Should you buy the work of contemporary artists? Yes, by all means. There is an excitement in owning contemporary art. It is of our time. A Cezanne need not hang beside a Degas. It may be in equally good company beside an American artist. And don't forget: the art of the masters was once contemporary.

If you have a traditionally decorated home, must you buy a traditional painting to fit in? No, no, a thousand times no! Art is not a decoration for a room. Decorate with ashtrays, vases, pillows. A picture is a work of art and stands by itself. It need only harmonize with you. No one can tell you what to buy, but if you can't afford a good oil painting or drawing by an artist you admire, buy a good original print by him.

MUGGLETON ART GALLERY   7 William St.   Auburn, N.Y. 13021   Dial 252-4433

"Central New York's Art Center for Original Prints and Fine Custom Framing"

Figure 25. An educational brochure on graphics; double fold, 8½ x 11 inches.

Our Gallery offers a

large selection of

Original Prints.

Chagall   Miro   Picasso

Rouault   Renoir   Baskin

Vasarely   Whistler   Goya

Durer   Rembrandt

and many others

Exclusive agent for all works
by Francoise Gilot.

The finest selection of matting
and museum framing in Central
New York.

Figure 26.
An educational
brochure on matting
and framing;
double fold,
8½ x 11 inches.

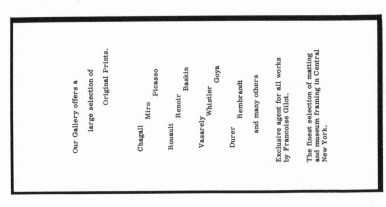

Are Your Fine Prints

Suffering

a Slow Death?

Muggleton Gallery
7 William Street
Auburn, New York 13021

IMPROPER MATTING AND FRAMING CAN LEAD TO PERMANENT DAMAGE TO YOUR FINE PRINTS AND DRAWINGS.

Many framers are not conscious of the deteriorating effects caused by the use of rubber cement, mounting tissue, masking tape, plastic tape, corrugated board and other impure materials.

The use of such framing materials is sometimes not apparent for several years because these damaging materials are completely hidden by framing. However there is a chemical reaction taking place between the impure mounting materials and the pure paper of a fine print. So by the time the damage is visible the print may have been permanently scarred. The result is not only unpleasant to view but, perhaps more important, the value of the drawing or print has been greatly decreased.

There are also many impure mat boards on the market today which "burn" the print along the opening, causing permanent damage to the print. The only safe matting board is "museum board", which is composed of high grade cellulose obtained from cotton fibers. "Museum board" should always be used next to the print, for the cut out mat as well as for backing.

Never place a print directly against the glass, since glass easily condenses moisture and may cause the growth of mold. Always use a mat which creates a "breathing space" between the picture and glass and allows the picture to move in response to changing atmospheric conditions. If the print is large and you do not wish the mat to show, the same protection can be provided by using a narrow strip of mat board that will be hidden beneath the inner edge of the frame.

When framing large modern prints it may be more practical to use Plexiglas instead of glass, since this is a better thermal insulator and will not condense moisture as easily as glass. Plexiglas is unbreakable and available with colorless additives that filter out damaging ultra-violet rays.

Never use "nonglare glass" on prints, drawings or watercolors as it tends to distort colors and diffuse the image.

Never place fine art pieces in direct sunlight or florescent lights as harmful rays cause bleaching, burning and general deterioration of the paper.

Paper is an organic substance that has its own beauty and life, and its specific qualities are integral to the print's aesthetic effect. Treat your prints with "tender loving care".

Oil paintings are subjected to deterioration caused by humidity, dryness, heat and chemical change. The damaging effects of drying and cracking can be corrected, or at least retarded, by proper cleaning and varnishing. This should be done at the first indication of dryness. Oil paintings should be professionally cleaned every few years, regardless of any apparent dryness or cracking.

We suggest you bring your framed prints, drawings, watercolors and oils to our gallery for an evaluation of condition and correction of any damage.

We will open your framed prints and check the condition of each print, examine the method of hinging and matting and give you a complete report on our examination.

There is no charge for this service. Stop in the gallery any day between the hours of 10 and 5 p.m., except Wednesdays or Sundays. If an evening appointment is more convenient please phone 252-4433.

8

SHOWS

The opening of an art show should have an air of festivity,
but even more, it should be dignified. An opening is the
time to build a favorable image for your gallery. The kind of
image you build will be determined by several factors: the
quality of the art, the knowledgeable manner in which you
respond to inquiries about the artists and their mediums,
the manner in which you have utilized the wall space and
floor space, the atmosphere you have created to make your
guests feel at home, and the cultural experience you have
provided for them as they view the exhibit.

Before discussing the different categories of shows,
there are several things that should be kept in mind. As
mentioned earlier, there will be times when an artist will not
be willing to pay all, or any part, of the expenses for his
show. In such a case you will have to decide just how much
you want to put on a show of the artist's work. In making
your decision you would do well to consider how his work
has sold while he has been on your roster, what prestige his
show will bring to your gallery, and how well known and established he is in the art world. If these things add up in the

artist's favor, you must then decide just how large a budget you are willing to allot for the show. It goes without saying that an artist in this category will usually dictate the type of invitation, brochure, publicity, and preview showing he expects. Under such circumstances, give all the ramifications a good deal of thought and try to determine what your gain will be before rashly spending an exorbitant amount on an opening. You should have an idea of the kind of budget needed for the show, and, unless you feel reasonably secure in the eventual return for the amount of money and energy expended, don't be over anxious.

I cannot be emphatic enough in reminding you that "artists are very important people." If you operate your gallery on a professional level, showing honesty and sincerity to all your artists, you will have twice the chance of achieving success in your gallery operation. Artists, both new and established, will find their way to your door even though you start out with a modest gallery. They will be willing to become affiliated with you if your reputation is one of reliability and integrity.

There are several types of shows, all the way from the one-man show, through the two or three-man show, to the group show, and even the guest-group show.

ONE-MAN SHOW

The number of artists in this type of show is self-explanatory by its title.

It is assumed that, once you have invited an artist to participate in a one-man show and have set the dates for the opening and the closing, you have also invited him to become a member of your "stable." And naturally, once you have gone so far as extending him this honor, let us assume that you have a verbal or written contract with him. Contractual agreements and contracts were discussed in Chapters 4 and 5, but let us discuss some points even further. As stated earlier, a contract could require the artist to pay all the expenses of his show. These expenses normally include publicity costs (newspaper advertising, TV and radio announcements, printing and mailing of invitations and brochures), transportation and insurance charges, and the cost of refreshments. The artist should be consulted as to how simple or how elaborate any of these should be if he is required to absorb the costs, since his ability and willingness to pay such expenses could dictate how simple or elaborate the invitations, brochures, and advertising are to be.

Some galleries include a percentage of their rent, heat, electricity, and employees' wages in the "costs" of an exhibition, but I do not feel this is a good policy. Such practice is frowned upon by honest, professional dealers, and most artists will shy away from a gallery that operates in this fashion.

Another way in which the expenses can be covered if the artist does not have the money but is willing to be responsible for such costs is for you to make an arrangement whereby you pay the costs and the artist gives you a number of pieces whose cost to you equals the sum of the expenses incurred. Such paintings, or whatever, would then belong to you in exchange for the costs involved in producing the exhibit. Naturally, you can only do this if you yourself are in a position to absorb the costs of an opening.

Once you have made all the necessary contractual arrangements you must make arrangements for selecting pieces for the show. One of the best ways of doing this is to go to the artist's studio and personally select what you feel is most suited for your clientele. This is not always possible, and if it is not, you can either view the artist's slides and rely on his judgment to make the final selection after you have made the preliminary selections from the slides, or the artist can bring his work to the gallery and at that time you can both make the selection.

As time goes on you will become experienced at judging the number of pieces needed to make an impressive exhibit. Of course, consideration must be given to the sizes of the pieces and the space available. It is a good idea, however, to have several pieces in your storeroom in addition to those exhibited, giving you the opportunity to rearrange the showing as pieces are sold.

Make suitable arrangements for delivery and allow ample time to guard against such unforeseen predicaments as loss or damage.

If possible, arrange to have the newspaper critics review the show prior to its opening. If you can work out this arrangement with all parties involved you will need the pieces in the gallery at a time determined by the newpaper reviewers. This could take place as many as two or three weeks before the opening. If you are fortunate enough to make such an arrangement, have everything efficiently prepared for

the critics when they arrive at the gallery: press releases
typed double spaced, glossy pictures of several pieces of the
artist's work (in case the newspaper does not bring a photographer), and the pieces ready for viewing. Arranging all of
this can be a difficult task because it means clearing an area
of the gallery and temporarily setting up the pieces for the
newspaper critics so that they will get a proper perspective
of the forthcoming exhibit. But there are times when it is
really worth it. If a good review appears in the newspapers
at the "propitious moment" (right before the opening of
the show), it can do more to stimulate sales than any amount
of paid advertising.

It is a good idea to have the artist present at the opening of his show if possible. Being able to advertise that the
artist will be present inspires greater interest on the part of
those who might be expected to view the works of art.

A word of caution is in order. If an artist works in
more than one medium, it is possible that you may not feel
his sculpture, for example, is on a par with his paintings.
You should reserve the right to refuse to exhibit that medium which you do not feel is on a par with his better medium.
Of course, it takes a bit of tact to communicate your decision. He should not really feel offended, if he realizes that
you have his best interests at heart as well as your own. Sales
would suffer as a result of exhibiting the poorer medium.
The viewer would hesitate to make a purchase after having
been unfavorably impressed by the "sculpture." It shouldn't
be so, but that, unfortunately, is human nature.

The manner in which the wall space and the floor space
is utilized can point out the difference between a profession-

al director and a non-professional one. Arranging the exhibit is of great importance. Remove all other artists' works from the "prime" space area (the part of the gallery used for publicized exhibits). If the show consists of paintings give a great deal of thought to their hanging. *Don't crowd* the pieces when arranging them. Large pieces are easier to arrange than smaller ones. Two or three large pieces can occupy one wall, but in the case of smaller pieces, arrange attractive groupings. But give each piece the opportunity to speak for itself. Putting too much on a wall is worse than too little.

TWO/THREE-MAN SHOW

The nature of this type of show is also self-explanatory by its title.

The same considerations will apply to the artist in a two/three-man show that apply to the artist in a one-man show, to this extent: the artists involved are likely to be members of your "stable" and have either written or verbal agreements with you.

It is a good idea to have a variety of artists, each of whom is well known, for different mediums. It makes for an interesting exhibit, for example, to have an oil painter, a sculptor, and an enamelist or ceramist participating in one show. Obviously, a multi-media two/three-man show will attract people interested in these different art forms. As a result, a greater number of people will attend the exhibit and, one hopes, provide a substantial number of sales.

Once the participating artists have been selected and the dates set for the opening and the closing, the next step is to decide on the kinds of invitations, brochures, publicity, and refreshments that are suitable and necessary for this kind of show (see Figures 27 and 28). Since more than one artist is involved, it is understandable that a larger budget must be planned than that involved in a one-man show. This is not to imply that the budget should be tripled, but rather that it will have to be a little bigger in order to allow a greater amount for the printing of brochures and invitations. A brochure and invitation involving three artists will contain more information than a brochure or invitation involving one artist.

Since it is next to impossible to meet with all the artists at one time, it is a good idea to estimate the overall cost of the exhibit and to divide it between the participants, assuring each that he will have equal billing. You should have an understanding that the suggested amount will have a degree of flexibility in the event of an unforeseen expenditure. Incidentally, it is very distasteful when either party to an arrangement is picayune, so be certain that you are not. If small costs arise unexpectedly don't make an issue over them. If the amounts are infinitesimal, absorb them yourself when you are involved with a two/three-man show.

Be cautious before offering to accept work from each artist in exchange for his share of the expenses in this type of show unless you are fairly certain of sales probabilities for the exhibit. As a matter of fact, you should give this matter considerable thought whenever you make this kind of arrangement, whatever the type of show.

111

The Painter's Mill Gallery

725 Park Avenue

PRESENTS A DUAL OPENING
OF WORKS BY

Edna Hibel

AND ENAMELIST

Max Karp

AN EXTENSIVE COLLECTION OF OVER 35 WORKS
BY EACH ARTIST WILL BE SHOWN

PREVIEW OPENING

Saturday, April 5, 1975
1 pm to 5 pm

EXHIBIT
Thru May 4, 1975

HOURS
Tuesday – Saturday 11 to 5
Sunday 1 to 5

Figure 27. Announcement of a two-man show; 5 x 7 inches.

Figure 28. Announcement of a four-man show; double fold, 10¼ x 14½ inches.

Making arrangements for selecting the pieces to be exhibited in a two/three-man show can take many days or even weeks. So be sure you allow ample time for delivery of the art.

GROUP SHOWS

A group show can provide the opportunity to exhibit the work of quite a few of the artists you represent. On the other hand, you may prefer to show a group of "guest" artists who are not members of your "stable" but whose work interests you.

The best time to schedule a group show or a guest-group show is in early December or in the slower months of May, June, and early September. If you are scheduling this type of show in early December you should select the lower-priced oils, prints, watercolors, drawings, ceramics, and jewelry that are especially appealing as Christmas gifts.

If the group show is to involve artists who are members of your "stable," chances are that you already have agreements with them. And if your agreement includes provisions relative to group shows, no further discussion is needed regarding expenses. It is a foregone conclusion that the expenses are to be shared equally by all the participating artists.

The same expense-sharing policy can be applied to guest-group shows as applies to group shows not involving guest artists. I have found, however, that guest artists are not too eager to contribute to a show when there is no guarantee that they will be included in your "stable" once the show is over. It would seem that it should be just the opposite—a guest artist should be anxious to make a contribution to get a "foot in the door," but it has been my experience that this is not so.

In the event that the artists are not willing to contribute toward a guest-group show it can still be worthwhile for you to pay the expenses of such a show because this type of an exhibit can have advantages for you. It brings new talent to your gallery and at the same time gives you the opportunity to expose this talent at a publicized show rather than merely placing the artists' work on display in the gallery.

Whether it be a "stable" group or guest-group show, one thing is certain—there is more work involved in this kind of show than in most other shows. You will not only have to select your artists far enough in advance to assure the best possible publicity (press releases and invitations) (see Figure 29), but you will have to select their work far enough in advance to assure prompt delivery to the gallery. A show of this type can begin to go into the planning stages as early as a year before its opening.

Even though I did not elaborate on wall space or floor space for any but the one-man show, one thing remains the same: "Arranging the exhibit is of great importance." Give it a great deal of thought. Don't crowd! Let each piece be important!

RECENT PAINTINGS
AND
SCULPTURE

FEBRUARY 10 – 28, 1976

KRAUSHAAR GALLERIES

Peggy Bacon	Al Fresco	watér color and ink
Ainslie Burke	Sand Beach	oil
Kenneth Callahan	Transition	tempera
David Cantine	Five Parts Still Life	acrylic
Leonard DeLonga	The Women	welded steel
Kenneth Evett	Portrait of Norman Daly	oil
Leon Goldin	September II	gouache
Tom Hardy	Bird	serpentine
John Hartell	Peconic	oil
John Heliker	Petunias and Blue Vase	oil
William Kienbusch	Atlantic Isle	casein
John Koch	Window Washers	oil
Robert Lahotan	House in Fog	oil

Figure 29. Announcement of a group show; single fold, artists listed on inside, gallery and dates on outside; 5 x 14½ inches.

Fred Laros	Another Island	collage and acrylic
Joe Lasker	Slanting Light	oil
Elsie Manville	Lazy Point Beach Heather	oil
Daniel O'Sullivan	At Tarquinii	oil
James Penney	Hallway Wall	oil
Andree Ruellan	Pomegranates	oil
Karl Schrag	Summer Bouquet with Straw Hat	oil
Jim Stark	Medallion #2	bronze
Jane Wasey	Turtle	granite
Jerome Witkin	Person Electric	oil

9

SHOWS OUTSIDE THE GALLERY

Many churches, synagogues, and community centers sponsor art shows and art auctions. They do this as a means of fund-raising. If you receive a request to perform such a service, don't disregard the invitation, especially when you are just getting your gallery started. Institutionally sponsored art events are excellent sources of free publicity. And further-more, such fund-raising functions are usually financially suc-cessful for the dealer as well as for the organization. If you accept a request to do a show or an auction for a nonprofit organization, it would be a good idea to attend some art shows and art auctions outside your community in order to get the feel of this particular type of operation before you attempt it yourself. If you cannot do this, however, the sug-gestions in this book should help you understand the me-chanics.

Before entering into a discussion concerning mechanics, I want to preface my remarks by saying that, whether it be a "show" or an "auction," the manner in which either is presented should be dignified. And the art exhibited should be of the same fine quality that is displayed in your gallery.

Do not bring in a lesser quality of art merely because you are directing a fund-raising event for a nonprofit organization.

When you are contacted by a group representing a church, synagogue, or community center with a request for an auction or a show, schedule a meeting as soon as possible with the committee in charge of the function for the purpose of discussing all the arrangements for the event. Here are some of the things that should be discussed: date and time, physical setup, lighting, identification method, record-keeping, commission, publicity, insurance, committee assistance, security, and refreshments.

Let us examine these points in greater detail.

DATE AND TIME

Before you set a date, try to determine what other events are taking place in your community. Choose a date when there is very little going on. Weekends are good for such functions. In the case of a synagogue, however, you will find Friday evening and all day Saturday prohibited because of the Sabbath. Therefore, it is best to schedule a synagogue art show so that it opens after sunset on Saturday and closes Sunday evening. It is important for you to know that a synagogue show planned for a Saturday night must be completely installed before sunset on Friday in order to open Saturday evening. Always check the time of sunset with the synagogue office, because it varies with the seasons. Scheduling events at churches is simpler for they are not bound by the aforementioned restrictions.

When you schedule a date and time for an auction, arrange a time for the preview showing and a time for the auction. For example, if an auction is scheduled to begin at 8:30 P.M. the doors should open for a preview showing at 6:00 P.M. The guests should be given the opportunity to view the works of art before the actual auction begins.

If you are located in "snow country" like Syracuse, New York, avoid scheduling either an art show or an art auction in the dead of winter. It is very difficult to load and unload your works of art under poor weather conditions. And in the event of a bad storm even the prospective buyers aren't very eager to brave the elements.

PHYSICAL SETUP FOR AN ART SHOW

Most churches, synagogues, and community centers have at least one large room and several smaller ones. Whenever possible, use the largest room and bring in as much art work as you can, in order to create an impressive display.

If the synagogue or church has its own display boards, or has another method of hanging pieces, then you are ahead of the game. But if they do not have proper equipment you will have to improvise your hanging method or procure display boards. Free-standing pegboards (4' x 8') with metal legs are usually available through "decorating" rental services. They can sometimes be borrowed from banks, libraries, other synagogues, or other churches. It is important, however, that you establish who will be responsible for supplying such equipment. Their rental can be costly. The responsibility for procuring such materials rarely falls to the gallery. It is usually the sponsoring organization that is responsible for procuring them.

Try to achieve interesting groupings. Mix the mediums and mix the price ranges when hanging the pieces. An attractive arrangement is one of the best vehicles for good sales.

A sculpture garden can be ingeniously arranged by adapting sewer pipes as pedestals, with pieces of slate placed on top. Wooden boxes, covered with burlap, and small barrels, attractively painted, also make interesting pedestals. A sculpture garden is most effective when placed near the entrance to the room or in the center of the display area. Don't hide it in some obscure corner.

Figure 30 provides an example of an art show outside the gallery. It was for the Hadassah Show at the Jewish Community Center in Wilkes-Barre, Pennsylvania. A great deal of ingenuity was used in hanging the wall and using the stage.

Figure 30. Example of an art show outside a gallery.

PHYSICAL SETUP FOR AN AUCTION

The physical setup for an auction is much simpler than the physical setup for an art show, but I would still suggest using a large room. Figure 31 can best illustrate one possible setup.

Paintings may be displayed by setting the bottom of a frame near the back edge of a table and allowing the piece itself to lean against the wall. Other pieces may be placed flat on the tables in front of those pieces that are leaning against the walls. Sculpture and pottery may be interspersed among the paintings. You will find it advantageous to display your pieces in numerical order. Both the auctioneer and the audience will find it easier if the catalog can be followed numerically.

Shows Outside the Gallery

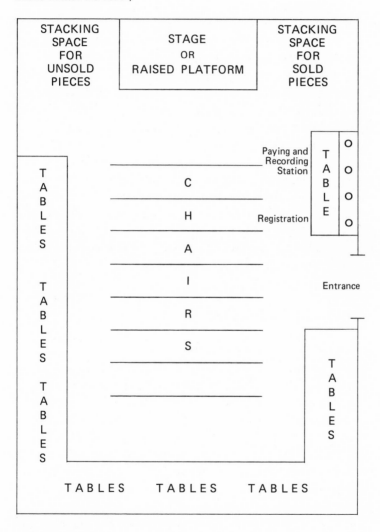

Figure 31. One way of setting up a room for an auction.

LIGHTING FOR AN ART SHOW

Churches, synagogues, and community centers do not usually have the type of lighting that will enhance works of art. For that reason it is almost always necessary to have additional lighting. Even though the lighting is your responsibility, it is often possible to find a committee member in the electrical business who is willing to be of assistance. I have found churches, as well as synagogues and community centers, with plenty of extension cords and lighting equipment; they very often have amateur productions of their own that require additional lighting. But check all this with the committee and don't leave anything to chance. Lighting should be given as much thought as hanging, because a work of art that is properly lit is greatly enhanced.

LIGHTING FOR AN AUCTION

As for lighting at an auction, the main consideration involves the stage or raised platform where the auctioneer holds forth. You will not be able to change lighting for different mediums while the auction is going on, and so you must optimize the effect that one type of lighting will have on the various mediums, especially those pieces covered with glass. I, therefore, suggest using "soft" spotlights and focusing the lighting so that there will be as little glare as possible. Check this from several places in the room and get it completely adjusted before the doors open for the preview. If you get the right light, you will get the maximum benefit of the lighting.

IDENTIFICATION OF PIECES FOR AN ART SHOW

There should be a simple catalog listing each piece (see Figure 32), and there should be a separate mimeographed brochure with short biographies of the artists. The gallery usually supplies these items, but there are some sponsoring organizations that prefer elaborate brochures, invitations, and catalogs and are willing to supply them (see Figures 33 and 34).

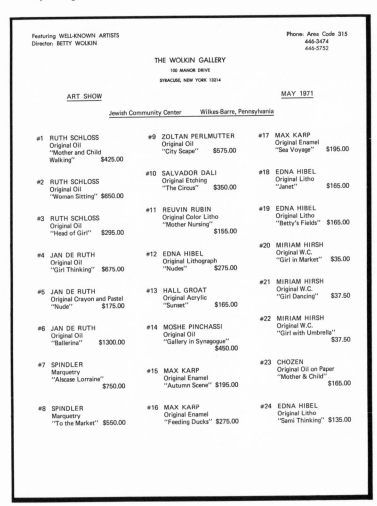

Featuring WELL-KNOWN ARTISTS
Director: BETTY WOLKIN

Phone: Area Code 315
446-3474
446-5752

THE WOLKIN GALLERY
100 MANOR DRIVE
SYRACUSE, NEW YORK 13214

ART SHOW

MAY 1971

Jewish Community Center   Wilkes-Barre, Pennsylvania

#1 RUTH SCHLOSS
Original Oil
"Mother and Child
Walking" $425.00

#2 RUTH SCHLOSS
Original Oil
"Woman Sitting" $650.00

#3 RUTH SCHLOSS
Original Oil
"Head of Girl" $295.00

#4 JAN DE RUTH
Original Oil
"Girl Thinking" $675.00

#5 JAN DE RUTH
Original Crayon and Pastel
"Nude" $175.00

#6 JAN DE RUTH
Original Oil
"Ballerina" $1300.00

#7 SPINDLER
Marquetry
"Alscase Lorraine"
$750.00

#8 SPINDLER
Marquetry
"To the Market" $550.00

#9 ZOLTAN PERLMUTTER
Original Oil
"City Scape" $575.00

#10 SALVADOR DALI
Original Etching
"The Circus" $350.00

#11 REUVIN RUBIN
Original Color Litho
"Mother Nursing"
$155.00

#12 EDNA HIBEL
Original Lithograph
"Nudes" $275.00

#13 HALL GROAT
Original Acrylic
"Sunset" $165.00

#14 MOSHE PINCHASSI
Original Oil
"Gallery in Synagogue"
$450.00

#15 MAX KARP
Original Enamel
"Autumn Scene" $195.00

#16 MAX KARP
Original Enamel
"Feeding Ducks" $275.00

#17 MAX KARP
Original Enamel
"Sea Voyage" $195.00

#18 EDNA HIBEL
Original Litho
"Janet" $165.00

#19 EDNA HIBEL
Original Litho
"Betty's Fields" $165.00

#20 MIRIAM HIRSH
Original W.C.
"Girl in Market" $35.00

#21 MIRIAM HIRSH
Original W.C.
"Girl Dancing" $37.50

#22 MIRIAM HIRSH
Original W.C.
"Girl with Umbrella"
$37.50

#23 CHOZEN
Original Oil on Paper
"Mother & Child"
$165.00

#24 EDNA HIBEL
Original Litho
"Sami Thinking" $135.00

Figure 32. Page from an art show catalog which included 329 works of art; 8½ x 11 inches.

*You Are Cordially Invited To Attend
A Gala Preview Cocktail Party For*

Hadassah's Art Show '74

*Saturday, November 2, 1974
7:30 - 11:00 p.m.*

*Jewish Community Center
60 South River St. - Wilkes-Barre, Pa.*

Exhibition & Sale

*Original Paintings & Sculpture
By World Renowned Masters and
Contemporary Artists*

*Donation for Gala Preview
$5.00 per person
R.S.V.P. by October 25, 1974*

*Sunday Hours
12 Noon to 10:00 p.m.
Open To Public*

Figure 33. Inside of single-fold invitation supplied by sponsoring organization; 7 x 10 inches.

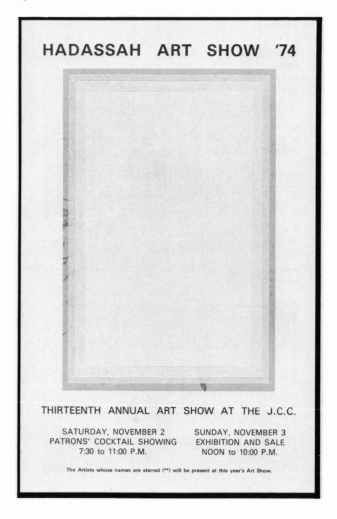

Figure 34. Cover and one inside page from an eight-page brochure of

ALVAR . . Spanish painter and lithographer . . exhibits superb craftsmanship in his unusual interplay of colors and the unique effects obtained by overprinting of stones . . His colors are rich, his subject matter varied, and a subtle sophisticated tenderness pervades his work.

MARILYN SICA . . American printmaker . . . studied in New York, Vietnam, Greece, and Yugoslavia . . Her strong and imaginative collographs and relief etch.. gs have brought her international attention. While her jewel-like works are evocative of the art and mythology of the ancient cultures of Asia and the Mediterranean, they convey a very contemporary feeling. Each of her works combines strong relief with coloring — sometimes bold, sometimes subtle. In British, French, Canadian and American Museum Collections.

SANDU LIBERMAN . . . Graduated from the Academy of Fine Arts in Bucharest. Honored with 11 one-man shows in Europe in 1952. He was official portrait painter of Rumania from 1962 - 1964 . . . His individual style is readily recognizable for its direct emotional appeal. His painter's vocabulary is as controlled as a fine raconteur's.

CHAIM GROSS . . is regarded as one of the foremost artists, sculptors, wood and stone carvers of our time. This superb artisan combines technical craftsmanship with the lyrical sensitivity that is the hallmark of his work. Born in March, 1904 in the Carpathian mountains of East Austria. He came to this country in 1921 where he studied at the Educational Alliance Art School, the Beaux Arts Institute and the Art Students League. He had a one-man show at the Whitney Museum of American Art. Mr. Gross won many prizes for sculpture from the Metropolitan Museum of Art, N. Y., Boston Arts Festival, Boston, Mass.; Pennsylvania Academy of Fine Arts, Philadelphia, Pa. The books that have been published about Chaim Gross are "Chaim Gross-Sculptor" by Josef Vincent Lombardo; "Fantasy Drawings" by Gross, with an introduction by Abraham L. Chanin and Dr. Samuel Atkin; "Four Expressionists" by Lloyd Goodrich, Director of the Whitney Museum. He is represented in more than 40 major museums throughout the U. S. and in Israel.

MICHEL DELACROIX . . Parisian art instructor and theatrical designer . . . His primitive-style paintings and lithographs combine structure and detail, plus rich color, to convey the bustling and diverse activity of Paris streets.

** JONATHAN TALBOT . . . painter and printmaker educated at Brandeis . . . etchings in a variety of subjects predominately handled with the precision and intensity of a Rembrandt. This "Renaissance" man is also well recognized in the musical field having appeared in Carnegie Hall. He has won many awards for his etchings and is a noted lecturer of printmaking and collecting.

JOHNNY FRIEDLAENDER . . Ranks as one of the top printmakers in Europe. The work produced in the Friedlaender atelier in Paris is today valued by museum curators and print collectors as the most exciting and original graphic art produced anywhere in the world. The technique — its intricate articulation of form speaks for itself. Here is a harmony of esthetics of which the most prominent modern artists would be proud.

artists' short biographies supplied by sponsoring organization; information supplied by gallery; 6 x 9½ inches.

131

Every piece of art should have its identifying number marked somewhere on the piece: back, front, top, or bottom. And every work of art should be identified by a card attached to the wall or pedestal with tape, close to the piece it is identifying (see Figure 35). The numbers marked on the pieces must correspond with the numbers on the cards, and both of these must be the same as the numbers in the catalog.

THE WOLKIN GALLERY

No.

Artist:

Title:

Medium:

Price:

Figure 35. Identification card for work of art; 3 x 4 inches.

IDENTIFICATION OF PIECES FOR AN AUCTION

A simple catalog (see Figure 36) should be distributed to the guests. It is not necessary to have a brochure with biographies of the artists. The auctioneer can give a short résumé of the artist whose work is up for bidding. If a purchaser insists on a written biography, one can always be mailed to him at a later date.

Every work of art should be labeled in a conspicuous place with the same number as shown in the catalog so that guests can follow the catalog at the preview as well as during the auction.

RECORD-KEEPING FOR A SHOW

A table with at least three hostesses should be set up at the entrance to the exhibition room. One person at the table may be in charge of seeing that guests write their names and addresses in your guest book. The other two hostesses will actually provide a paying station plus security. This station and its attendants will make certain that payment has been made for all works of art removed from the premises.

There should be ample hosts and/or hostesses to act as salespersons. Each salesperson should have a three-copy sales book. When a guest makes a purchase, a sales slip should be made out in triplicate, with the following information: name and address of purchaser, artist's name, title of work, medium, number of piece, and price. The salesperson should

Featuring WELL-KNOWN ARTISTS
Director: BETTY WOLKIN

Phone: Area Code 315
446-3474
446-5752

THE WOLKIN GALLERY

ART AUCTION

CATALOGUE

100 MANOR DRIVE

SYRACUSE, NEW YORK 13214

1 SANDU LIBERMAN ORIGINAL OIL The Western Wall	2 SANDU LIBERMAN ORIGINAL OIL The Scribe	3 JOSEPH FAHRI ORIGINAL OIL Lonely Tree
4 JOSEPH FAHRI ORIGINAL OIL Landscape	5 JOSEPH IJAKY ORIGINAL POLYMER To the Marketplace	6 AHUVA SHERMAN ORIGINAL OIL A City is Born
7 YEHUDA RODAN ORIGINAL OIL The Western Wall	8 CHAIM ADLER ORIGINAL BRASS RELIEF The Trio	9 JOSEPH AMITY ORIGINAL OIL City
10 RUTH SCHLOSS ORIGINAL OIL Girl	11 SANDU LIBERMAN ORIGINAL OIL Village Beauty	12 HENRY ORIGINAL OIL A Breath of Spring
13 JOSEPH FAHRI ORIGINAL OIL Bar Kochba	14 JOSEPH FAHRI ORIGINAL Kiddush	15 ITZHAK MESHER ORIGINAL OIL
16 ITZHAK MESHER ORIGINAL OIL	17 ITZHAK MESHER ORIGINAL OIL	18 ITZHAK MESHER ORIGINAL OIL
19 HENRY ORIGINAL OIL Spring Bouquet	20 YEHUDA VARDI ORIGINAL OIL Boy	21 ZVI RAPHAELI ORIGINAL OIL Raising the Torah
22 RUDOLPH SEINWELL ORIGINAL OIL Contentment	23 M. KRAMER ORIGINAL OIL and MIXED MEDIA - Eternal Light	24 M. KRAMER - ORIGINAL OIL and MIXED MEDIA Traditions

ALL   SALES   FINAL

Figure 36. Page from an art auction catalog that included 126 works of art; 8½ x 11 inches.

give two copies (original and second) to the buyer who will then take these two copies to the "paying station" at the entrance to the room. One hostess at the table should accept payment for the work and mark both copies of the sales slip "paid." The other hostess should check the calculations on the sales slip, give one copy to the customer, file the other copy in a small metal card-file box, and mark the piece "sold" on her copy of the catalog. The buyer will then take the "paid" sales slip back to the salesperson, who will either remove the piece of art and give it to the new owner, or put a "sold" sticker on the piece and make an arrangement for the painting, or whatever, to be picked up at the close of the show.

There are differences of opinion on whether to give the purchaser his work of art at the time it is purchased or have him pick it up after the show. Many gallery directors prefer not to have their hanging disturbed, but I prefer to give the buyer his piece of art at the time the purchase is made and then rehang and rearrange the show at the end of the first day. It has never failed (for me, that is) that whenever I have placed a "sold" sticker on a work of art there is no other piece that will satisfy the next buyer.

RECORD-KEEPING FOR AN AUCTION

You will need the following supplies:

1. 8" x 10" cardboards stencilled with large black numbers. Begin with number one and prepare more than you think you will need.

2. 3" x 5" or 4" x 6" cards on which to record each guest's identification number, name, address, and phone number.

3. Card-file box with alphabetical or numerical insert.

4. Salesbook in triplicate.

5. Master sheet on which to record the guest's identification number, name, and address.

(Incidentally, it is more efficient if your cards, file box, and sales slips are all about the same size.)

As each guest (or family) comes into the room the hostess at the registration table should give him an 8" x 10" card with a number on it; this is referred to as the guest's identification number (see Figure 37). The hostess should then fill out a card with the guest's I.D. number, name, address, and phone number (see Figure 38). She should then pass this card to one of the hostesses at the paying and recording station, who should record the guest's I.D. number, name, and address on a master sheet (see Figure 39). The card should then be filed in the file box, either numerically or alphabetically.

You will need several hostesses to act as "runners":

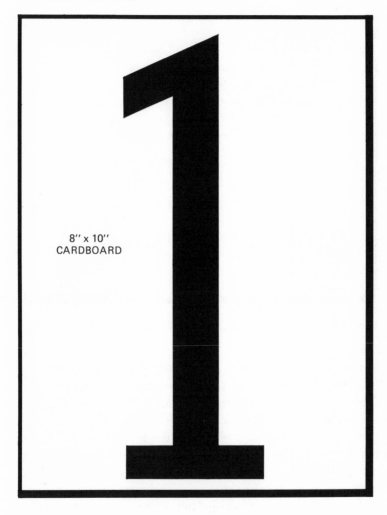

8'' x 10''
CARDBOARD

Figure 37. Guest's identification number at an auction; 8½ x 11-inch card.

MR. & MRS. JOHN DOE   I.D. # 1
100 LONG LANE
SYRACUSE N.Y. 13205
PHONE 423-4567

Figure 38. Guest's registration card at an auction; 4 x 6 inches.

one or two to bring the works of art to the stage for auc-
tioning, and one or two to take the auctioned pieces from
the auctioneer to either the stacking space for "sold" pieces
or to the stacking space for "unsold" pieces. If you have displayed your art numerically, have the pieces brought to the
auctioneer in their numerical order. This makes it easier for
the guests and the hostesses to follow the catalog. It also
makes it easier for the "runners"; they can stack both the
sold and the unsold pieces in their numerical order, thereby
making it simpler for a hostess to locate a piece when a
buyer is ready to pick it up.

Figure 39. Master sheet at an auction.

You are best qualified to act as your own auctioneer. You are respected as the gallery director and you are familiar with the art and the artists. Don't be inhibited. You don't have to sound like a tobacco auctioneer. You will, however, have to find a way to capture your audience in order to get them to participate, since you will not be dealing with a group of professional buyers. You'll have to use a little bit of the "ham" we all are endowed with in order to get the desired result, but anyone with any ingenuity can do it very nicely. Once you have put your audience at ease you can proceed. A simple, straightforward, short biography of the artist, followed by the lowest acceptable opening bid, is all that is really needed to get the bidding started. "How to Run an Art Auction" is reprinted here by permission of *Art Material Trade News,* March 1972:

How to Run
An Art Auction

Sir, if you're waving, you're bidding!" The gavel falls and the art auction is underway.

Art material dealers who have a gallery and frame shop may well take a leaf from Jean Richards' success book and pick up some additional income via an art auction. It's a lot of fun, a lot of work and can lead to handsome profits for an alert auctioneer.

Jean Richards, who owns the *J. Richards Gallery, Inc.* in Englewood, N.J., has been pounding her gavel at some 70 sales parties a year for the past several years and she loves every minute of it. Last month she held a typical auction at Temple Avoda in Fair Lawn, N.J. It made a very interesting Sunday afternoon.

There was a lot of good art at the auction, but only a few works by really big names: Chagall, Picasso, Miro, etc. Miss Richards explains her stance quite logically: "We have finer quality art than when we started a few years ago because we don't concentrate on the biggest names. At auction prices, we could offer only lesser works of the masters. Now we can offer the very finest examples by up and coming young American artists." The sales tended to hang in clumps around $50 and slightly over $100.

It sounds quite simple: the gallery buys works of art outright from artists, from *Associated American Artists*, from *Hammer Galleries* and other sources. Her shop frames them, using a lot of sectional frames and carved Mexican jobs. A dealer contemplating a similar venture might well work with art on consignment as Jean Richards did when she got started. Now she finds it advantageous to buy, and with her turnover, she can negotiate a better price.

A charitable organization sponsors the event, does the publicity and provides the space for the auction. Some charge admission for the viewing, some maintain a snack bar and baby sitters, others open the doors to all and offer a raffle. The sponsor gets a flat 20 per cent off the top. Obviously each work has an opening bid which covers costs and allows the gallery owner a minimal profit. If there are no bids at the price, the painting is knocked down for some other auction later.

There is no nonsense in the procedure; it is not a social affair. Her patter goes something like this: "Number three is a beautiful floral done with a palette knife. Show it to the right and then show it to the people on the left. We are opening this stunning still life at $35, framed and ready to hang. Are there any bids at $35? No one seems interested so we'll move on to the next one. Will you bring out the Edna Hibel? Now here we have a signed and numbered original lithograph by America's foremost woman artist. . . ."

And so it goes for an entire afternoon. Of the 150 works shown, slightly over half were purchased, generally after three or four bids. For the sponsor, it is a clean way to make money: no need for endless committees and hours or work preparing a baked bean supper at small profit. The sponsor in this case, Temple Avoda, was backing Jean Richards for the second time. The first year's profit for the Temple was around $1100. The second time around it went up to perhaps $12-1300. Obviously a small market reaches a saturation point, and Temple Avoda may well let a year pass before doing it again. Barbara Bolton, committee chairman, was very pleased with the results and had only praise for the efficiency and dispatch in setting up the pegboard display by the J. Richards crew. The Temple gets solicitations from half a dozen galleries a year, suggesting this type of fund raising. All checks are made out to the Temple, which then pays the gallery.

Jean Richards, meanwhile, is off to green fields in the Midwest almost before the current auction is dismantled and returned to the shop. She has the Kidney Foundation and Holy Name Hospital coming up, is off to hold an auction in mid-air aboard a 747, did one at the Mental Health Assn.'s black tie dinner and has plans for an invasion of the untapped Midwest, America's most fertile fields.

If you do not have your own assistants at the paying and recording station, request the sponsor's committee to select a group of hosts and hostesses that are not only very alert people but also very quick with figures or a pocket calculator. Arrange a briefing session in advance and acquaint them with the procedures they will be required to follow. The following system is very effective, provided the auctioneer is very clear and provided the hostesses follow the auctioneer very carefully. When the auctioneer gives forth with, "Going! Going! Gone! Number one in the catalog, a Sandu Liberman oil, goes to number one hundred thirty-two for two hundred and fifty dollars," one hostess at the recording table should mark her catalog accordingly (see Figure 40). Another hostess should make out a sales slip—in triplicate—with the following information: I.D. number, name, and address of the buyer (taken from the master sheet), catalog number, title, and selling price. The third hostess should check the sales slip and file all three copies in back of the purchaser's registration card in the card-file box.

When the buyer comes to the paying station to pay for his new acquisitions, a hostess merely has to locate his card. His sales slip, or slips, will be right in back of his registration card. Upon payment, the hostess should mark all three copies "paid," give the original copy to the new owner, and retain the other two copies: one for the organization and one for your records. The buyer can present his "paid" sales slip to the hostess stationed where the "sold" pieces have been stacked and pick up his purchase.

The people who buy at an auction are either "quick buyers," "impulse buyers," or "knowledgeable buyers." There are others, however, who would like to buy but are too timid to make a fast commitment. They will sometimes wait until after the auction to approach you and ask if they can purchase an unsold piece at the opening bid. This is perfectly legitimate. The only problem you may have in such a case is that a particular piece could have been opened below

143

Featuring WELL-KNOWN ARTISTS
Director: BETTY WOLKIN

Phone: Area Code 315
446-3474
446-5752

THE WOLKIN GALLERY

ART AUCTION

100 MANOR DRIVE

CATALOGUE

SYRACUSE, NEW YORK 13214

1 SANDU LIBERMAN   #132
   ORIGINAL OIL
   The Western Wall $250⁰⁰

2 SANDU LIBERMAN
   ORIGINAL OIL
   The Scribe

3 JOSEPH FAHRI
   ORIGINAL OIL
   Lonely Tree

4 JOSEPH FAHRI
   ORIGINAL OIL
   Landscape

5 JOSEPH IJAKY
   ORIGINAL POLYMER
   To the Marketplace

6 AHUVA SHERMAN
   ORIGINAL OIL
   A City is Born

7 YEHUDA RODAN
   ORIGINAL OIL
   The Western Wall

8 CHAIM ADLER
   ORIGINAL BRASS RELIEF
   The Trio

9 JOSEPH AMITY
   ORIGINAL OIL
   City

10 RUTH SCHLOSS
    ORIGINAL OIL
    Girl

11 SANDU LIBERMAN
    ORIGINAL OIL
    Village Beauty

12 HENRY
    ORIGINAL OIL
    A Breath of Spring

13 JOSEPH FAHRI
    ORIGINAL OIL
    Bar Kochba

14 JOSEPH FAHRI
    ORIGINAL
    Kiddush

15 ITZHAK MESHER
    ORIGINAL OIL

16 ITZHAK MESHER
    ORIGINAL OIL

17 ITZHAK MESHER
    ORIGINAL OIL

18 ITZHAK MESHER
    ORIGINAL OIL

19 HENRY
    ORIGINAL OIL
    Spring Bouquet

20 YEHUDA VARDI
    ORIGINAL OIL
    Boy

21 ZVI RAPHAELI
    ORIGINAL OIL
    Raising the Torah

22 RUDOLPH SEINWELL
    ORIGINAL OIL
    Contentment

23 M. KRAMER
    ORIGINAL OIL and MIXED
    MEDIA - Eternal Light

24 M. KRAMER - ORIGINAL
    OIL and MIXED MEDIA
    Traditions

ALL   SALES   FINAL

Figure 40. Art auction catalog recording number of person to whom piece was sold and its price; 8½ x 11 inches.

cost in order to get the audience primed. Nevertheless, I am inclined to accommodate such "timid" people. It is for this reason that you must be very careful in calculating the opening prices on all your pieces. Remember that your cost is actually your original cost plus the commission you will have to pay the organization.

Even though "all sales are final" you should maintain a certain degree of flexibility. If any unforeseen situation arises, just use good judgment and adopt the policy that you must "Satisfy the buyer at *almost* any cost."

COMMISSIONS

The commission paid to the organization is the same whether the event is an auction or a sale. The amount is usually 20 percent of the total sales. This may seem like a large slice of the pie, but what is given away in commission is made up for in volume.

PUBLICITY

Publicity is always the responsibility of the sponsoring institution (see Figure 41 for an example of a poster distributed by a Rochester, New York synagogue at their own expense). However, because they are nonprofit organizations, synagogues, churches, and community centers have very little trouble getting free publicity. Television "Ladies

Figure 41. Double-fold poster distributed by a sponsoring organization at its own expense; 11 x 20 inches, outside used for address.

146

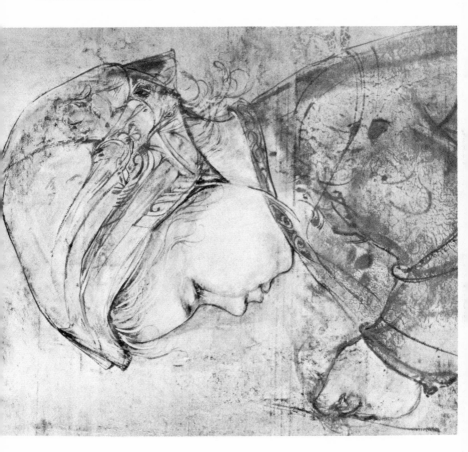

Shows" are the ones most willing to have such groups as part of their programs. They are pleased to feature a community event on these shows. If a television program can be arranged, volunteer to go to the TV station with one or two of the committee members. Take several colorful paintings with you. Such programs are done either live or taped. Try to have your event appear on television three or four days before the actual date of the function.

Newspapers are especially kind to such organizations. They are usually happy to print a picture of the committee together with several works of art (see Figures 42 and 43 for examples of some of the free newspaper publicity that was given to nonprofit charitable groups sponsoring art exhibitions).

At this point I cannot resist the temptation to tell an unbelievable story. It didn't happen to me, but it did happen to one of my friends. A newspaper photographer requested a painting so that he could photograph it and use it for the article he was doing about her art show at a church. He even offered to stop at the gallery and select a piece he felt would be most photogenic. When he arrived at the gallery, my friend and an artist were going over some unframed pieces that were painted on masonite. The photographer fell in love with one particular piece. He insisted that it didn't matter that the piece was unframed. He said he could take care of the situation during the printing process. So the artist agreed to let the newspaper photographer borrow the painting. The following day the photographer called my friend and said, "That painting is a little too big. I wish it could be printed a little smaller but I guess that would destroy the esthetic effect."

BRIGHTONIANS Mrs. Leo Hochhauser (left) and Mrs. Stanley Levinson plan Beth Sholom art exhibit and sale.

Beth Sholom Women To Have Art Exhibit

The Sisterhood of Beth Sholom Congregation will have an art exhibit and sale Sunday from 2 to 11 p.m. and Monday from 11 a.m. to 4 p.m. in the synagogue, 1161 Monroe Ave.

Mrs. Stanley Levinson of 81 Rockhill Rd., Brighton, said a select and diversified collection of paintings from the Wolkin Galleries of Syracuse will be featured.

* * *

Included in the exhibit will be paintings by such artists as Edna Hibel, Hall Groat, Edward Elhoff, Paula Nasselli, Ruvin Rubin, Ruth Schloss, Sander Liberman, Mariano Ortuzar, Max Karp, John E. Detore, Yehuda Vardi, Moshe Pinchasi and also Batik by Nan.

The exhibit and sale will be arranged and directed by Mrs. Levinson assisted by Mrs. Moe Schreiber of 63 Tarrytown Rd., Brighton, and Mrs. Leo Hochhauser, 68 Warrington Dr., Brighton, co-chairman.

Hostesses will be Mrs. Sol Shulman, Mrs. Irving Goldstein, Mrs. Eli Fix, Mrs. Louis Garden, Mrs. William Lieberman, Mrs. Chester Stein, Mrs. Jerry Brovitz, Mrs. Harold Slavny, Mrs. Maurice Soloman, Mrs. Morton Goldberg, Mrs. Henry Hoschander, Mrs. Irving Wietschner, Mrs. Mollie Spiegelman, Mrs. Gerald Usdane, Mrs. Leo Rudin, Mrs. Ben Kaplan, Mrs. Irving Disraeli, Mrs. Bernard Bachman and Mrs. Abe Berzansky.

Figure 42. Example of free newspaper publicity.

Hadassah's Gala Art Show Previewed at JCC Last Night

It might have been the Museum of Modern Art in New York or the Corcoran Gallery in Washington, but it was not—it was the Jewish Community Center last night which provided the setting for the gala preview cocktail party heralding the opening of Hadassah's Art Show '74.

The walls of the center were covered with every type of painting as well as excellent pieces of sculpture and other art objects.

As the guests milled around, they enjoyed cocktails and hot canapes served from strategically placed tables throughout the room.

It was an elegant affair with women wearing Fall clothes and members in particular acting as hostesses for the occasion at which several hundred were present.

The show will be opened today from 12 noon until 10 p.m. and the public is invited to browse and to buy from the original paintings of the world-renowned masters and contemporary artists.

Particularly in evidence was a Wilkes-Barre native Sam Savitt, who was born and reared in the Heights Section.

Mr. Savitt has been making news in art circles for the past 15 years because of his paintings of horses. He is the official artist of the U.S. Equestrian Team and has done work for Sports Illustrated, America's national sports weekly.

Son of the late Mr. and Mrs. Hyman Savitz (Sam whose last name's spelling was changed from "Z" to "T" by a publisher), still retains close contacts in this area.

He is the cousin of Abe Savitz, Atty. Joseph Savitz, Joseph S. Savitz, Sam Savitz, Mrs. Murray Popky, Mrs. Leonore Kornfeld, Mrs. Sophie Weinstock, and is the nephew of Mrs. Sarah Savitz.

The author-illustrator (Sam has had several books published including the famed "Around the World With Horses") is not only an artist but with his wife and two children, a devoted horseman.

He is a graduate of Pratt Institute but readily told the guests last night that his first contact with horses took place when he was a youngster of 11 living in the Heights. He nearly drowned when he attempted a cowboy stunt the first time he mounted a horse.

Well, "My mother made me get right back on and my love for the graceful animal began."

Drawing horses runs in the family. Sam has a brother Alfred who also does a bang-up job of "handling horseflesh" on the drawing board. He specializes in illustrating action stories dealing with horses and these appear in cowboy publications of all types.

Many of the artists were present to discuss their works and the evening was a tremendous success.

The tone of the show will be less casual today but equally as much fun.

Figure 43. Example of free newspaper publicity with art in background of photo.

"That's O.K." said my friend, "go ahead and crop it."

I know you'll find this hard to believe, but he "cropped" it alright! Not the photograph! The painting! And by three inches, no less! Thank heaven the artist had a sense of humor. But you might not find many artists with such a sense of humor, so be careful.

INSURANCE

The organization should be very specific as to the insurance coverage they plan to carry for this type of function. You can then discuss everything with your insurance broker to ascertain what, if any, additional coverage you might need for the event.

COMMITTEE ASSISTANCE

An art show or an art auction outside your own gallery is a big undertaking, but the burden is reduced considerably when you have the help and cooperation of the sponsor's committee members. You will need many volunteers. It is a good idea to have the chairperson set up a time schedule for the workers. Go over this with her so that you will be sure of enough help at the right time.

SECURITY

If the organization does not have its own security system I
would suggest that security be arranged on a twenty-four-
hour basis. This can be costly, so have an understanding regarding this expense. I usually split such costs with the organization.

REFRESHMENTS

Refreshments are entirely the responsibility of members of
the committee. If they decide to serve refreshments it is best
to use a separate room specifically for this purpose.

10

APPRAISING AND FRAMING

APPRAISING

Appraising works of art may necessitate your having pieces
on your premises that do not belong to you. I would suggest
you discuss this with your insurance broker and make arrangements to have additional coverage when such a situation arises. It may merely entail a phone call to your broker
when a piece comes in and another phone call when it goes
out. It is almost certain to take days or even weeks to re-
search a piece with which you are not familiar. If, during
such time, it should be stolen or damaged you might possibly incur a liability.

If you are called upon to appraise a work of art with
which you are not familiar, make a record, in duplicate, on
gallery stationery while the client is in the gallery and include the following information: the date, the client's name
and address, the artist's name, the medium, the size (with
and without frame), and if sculpture, whatever measure-
ments best describe the size (length, width, height), the
condition of the piece, whether it is signed or unsigned,

where signature is located, and the price paid by the client. Give one copy to the client and keep one for your records. Having a record of a piece left for appraisal can be a big help in the event of loss or damage. Furthermore, in appraising such works of art it is a good idea to seek the assistance of a specialist when you do not feel secure in your own judgment.

A good source of information for appraisal purposes is Art Appraisal and Information, Art Reference Gallery, Inc., 89 Park Street, Montclair, New Jersey, 07042. In order to avail yourself of their services it is necessary to become a member of the organization. The yearly dues are very low for the many services offered—$20 per year as of this writing. There is a small charge for each appraisal—in addition to the yearly dues—but it is well worth it. You can depend on this organization to research any work of art and send you a true appraisal. You can include their charges when you calculate your charge to your client.

The fee for appraisals should be commensurate with the time and money spent to arrive at the current value of the work being appraised, but I never charge more than 5 percent of the value. On the other hand, a minimum fee of $15 is not unreasonable.

Inform your clients if a piece they have purchased from you has increased in value. Any client will be thrilled to have a note saying: "I am pleased to inform you that your Edna Hibel lithograph titled 'Mother and Three Children' has increased in value by 25 percent. Should you desire to increase your insurance coverage on the abovementioned lithograph, this note can serve as an official appraisal."

I have made it a practice not to charge my clients for a reappraisal on pieces that are purchased from me regardless of the amount of time that has elapsed between the purchase and the time of the new appraisal.

FRAMING

The best method of servicing your clients in this area, unless you plan to have a complete frame shop in addition to the gallery, is to make an arrangement with a framer. Have him supply you with corner samples of moldings and corner samples of colored mats. Most people have difficulty visualizing a piece before it is framed, but the corner moldings and corner mats enable you to offer your clients ideas and enable them to visualize the "finished product." Furthermore, the customer does not have to be bothered taking the piece elsewhere.

Even though picture-framing today is big business, there is plenty of bad framing around. Make certain your framer is interested in more than just producing mass framing. He should be more interested in enhancing a work of art.

Insist that he use only "Rag Stock" when framing prints because the high acid content in regular paper can damage a work of art over a period of years.

The framer will teach you his method for calculating the price of a frame so that you can give the client the total price of a finished job. Most frame shops give a gallery a rebate of 25 percent of the total price of the frame.

ONE PARTING THOUGHT

Sincerity, integrity and a love of art are basic requisites for the development and success of an art gallery. Be gentle and dignified in your approach. Don't ever high-pressure a client! Let the work speak for itself. Don't sell any work of art unless you yourself are happy with it. Don't sell a work of art unless the client is completely satisfied with it.

I hope that *Gallery Management* has broadened your insight and understanding of the scope and ramifications of owning and operating an art gallery.

GALLERY MANAGEMENT

was composed in 12-point IBM Selectric Bodoni Book and leaded one point
by Metricomp Studios;
with display type handset in Bodoni Modern by Dix Typesetting Co., Inc.;
printed offset on Warren 55-pound Antique Cream and
bound over boards in Columbia Bayside Chambray
by Vail-Ballou Press, Inc.;
and published by

SYRACUSE UNIVERSITY PRESS

Syracuse, New York 13210